Birdsong

For John ([illegible])
with all good wishes,
Dewi Roberts

Birdsong

Compiled by Dewi Roberts

Foreword by Jon Gower

seren

Seren is the book imprint of
Poetry Wales Press Ltd
Nolton Street, Bridgend, Wales
www.seren-books.com

ISBN 1-85411-326-7

A CIP record for this title is available from the British Library

The publisher acknowledges the financial assistance
of the Arts Council of Wales

Printed in Plantin by Bell & Bain, Glasgow

Cover photograph by Mark Hamblin, rspb-images.com

Contents

BIRDS OF PREY

SEA BIRDS

LAKE AND RIVER BIRDS

THE CROW FAMILY

LARKS

CAGE BIRDS

MISCELLANY

Foreword

It just might be that bird poetry, like the bittern, Siberian crane or Spinx's macaw is endangered. If you peruse many a new anthology of verse you'll find that poets address the urban world or the inner world, seldom penning a nature poem. Dewi Roberts' anthology tilts this balance back, with words about birds winging from centuries ago to join busy flocks of recent verse.

Dewi Roberts, whose fingers must be slightly stiff by now after turning quite so many pages, has also garnered a respectable collection of prose, from Christopher Meredith's courtly novel, *Griffri* to Brenda Chamberlain's Bardsey island experiences. He also doesn't forget the naturalists, such as Ronald Lockley and Bill Condry, whose patience and quiet skill in the field was matched by the clarity of their writing.

In the anthology you can watch birds, carve models of them and trap moments of their flight. Here are chattering gatherings of birds – melody-makers, miraculous migrants and sometimes murderers. There are prison poems, such as the little hymn to a sparrow written from a cell in Swansea prison – which brings to mind the story of Branwen, or the Birdman of Alcatraz – but most often the bird is a symbol of freedom, of soaring independence.

This is a collection as varied and wonderful as the world of birds itself. It fair pulses with energy, like the steady metronome-beat of geese overhead, heading for winter haunt or summer home.

Jon Gower, 2002

Introduction

For centuries birds have had a universal significance in mythology, art and literature. The freedom of flight is frequently employed as a metaphor for an idealised human state, while the phoenix powerfully symbolises the ability, despite all the odds, to overcome defeat. This anthology offers abundant evidence of the constant stimulus which birds continue to provide to both poets and prose writers in Wales. It is a stimulus first recorded in *The Mabinogion*, in the tales of Branwen and Blodeuwedd, the potency of which continues to inspire many contemporary artists – poets, novelists, dramatists, film-makers, painters and sculptors. Between the bulk of this anthology, which is written in the Twentieth century, and *The Mabinogion*, lies a rich vein of literary birds. Giraldus Cambrensis writes of the eagle of Eryri, which ate the flesh of human corpses and almost perforated a rock in sharpening its beak. In the thirteenth century it seems that the seagull was the poets' messenger of choice: both Dafydd ap Gwilym, famously, and Llywelyn Goch ap Meurig use the bird to convey their love to their cariads. More darkly, Thomas Pennant was haunted by a mass of sea bird corpses some five centuries later.

The past also looms in some contemporary writing. Notably, in his novel *Griffri*, Christopher Meredith explores the superstition of the medieval period and the notion that a man's soul could enter a bird. This relationship between man and bird shifts from superstition to psychology as the centuries pass. Leslie Norris writes memorably of a poultry farmer who suffers a visitation by a flock of "great invisible birds", an experience which results in his becoming psychotic. The bird as cypher dates back centuries, as Vuyelwa Carlin describes in her poem about Icarus. More immediately, in historical terms and a personal sense, T.E. Nicholas, imprisoned on spurious charges because of his political beliefs, befriended a sparrow and in a poem to the bird writes about religious faith and freedom. Later, Idris Davies calls on the people of the industrialised valleys to send out their homing pigeons "...with messages tied to their wings,/ words of your anger, words of your love" in a poem which draws on the south Wales hobby of pigeon-fancying and is also a politicised echo of the medieval seagulls. Birds are similarly used as cultural cyphers in the Welsh-speaking heartlands. When that committed birdwatcher R.S. Thomas describes his sense of loss the year migratory birds did not fly over Llŷn, their absence becomes a metaphor for the precarious status of the Welsh language, while Gwilym R. Jones writes of the gander "Who gave the few quills to Bishop Morgan/ Giving the haven of its wings to the Welsh language". And it falls to Menna Elfyn to make a connection with which many writers will have sympathy, the bird as inspiration, when she compares the muse to

> The littlest of birds,
> a wren, unobserved
> in a dark wood.

Not surprisingly, perhaps, many of the poems and extracts of prose in the anthology are primarily celebratory, the original and most long standing human response to birds. Gerard Manley Hopkins, Dylan Thomas, Jim Perrin and Gwyneth Lewis lead the way here, the latter observing that

> Talon and claw
> are tender to me, the craw
>
> much kinder than men.

No doubt it is song and flight which most fascinate humans. The song of the thrush or nightingale, for instance, is a graphic reminder of the beauty and complexity of nature, and the grace and freedom of birds in flight are suggestive of aspects of spirituality in a world in which the purely material sometimes seems in danger of taking over our lives. When humans and birds attempt to co-exist the result can sometimes be catastrophic for the birds. While I was growing up in the Welsh countryside, the corncrake lost its battle with the new harvesting machines. Within the last few years an encouraging example of a reversal of that type of situation has occurred on the remote uplands of north Wales where an application to site a wind farm was rejected purely on the grounds that hen harriers have returned to use the area as a nesting ground. There are some two hundred red kites in Wales which are now able to breed without the previously rigid security surveillance which was once in force.

I hope this anthology may remind the reader of the immense pleasure and inspiration which can be derived through the preservation of the balance between ourselves and the abundance of every species of bird life.

Dewi Roberts, 2002

In the Beginning was the Bird

Before man, a bird,
a feather before time,
And music growing
outward into space...

Henry Treece

In The Beginning Was The Bird

In the beginning was the bird,
A spume of feathers on the face of time,
Man's model for destruction, God's defence.

Before man, a bird, a feather before time,
And music growing outward into space,
The feathered shears cutting dreams in air.

Before birds, a God, a Nothing with a shape
More horrible than mountains or the Plague,
A Voice as large as fate, a tongue of bronze.

Before this, O no before was there.
Where? Among the placeless atoms, mad
As tale the maggot makes locked in the skull.

And so I state a bird. For sanity
My brain's lips blow the tumbled plume.
I see it prophesy the path winds take.

Alison Bielski

The Birds

I

In the last days, a great wind sprang up,
hurtled across land and ocean.
A scorching wind singeing green hills,
sweeping men off their feet, it
battered crops, farms and houses,
scarring its path with crashing trees.

II

When they felt the first sighing of
disturbed leaves, birds called to each
other. This was the final freedom
they had been promised at creation.

They flew away with joyous singing,
timid and fierce, small and great,
squawking with delight, as twigs spun
through approaching storm winds, up,
up into pale sky towards the silent
storm centre, awaiting their liberation.

Then winds rose higher, blasting grass
and every living thing with burning
breath. Only insects crept deeper under
moist earth, wriggling in dark shelters.

III

Birds spun in that still storm centre,
wide wings outspread, chattering plans
to build new nests after the storm, to
strut fearlessly upon bare branches,
under fallen trees, in wide fields,
where no animal would molest them.

They knew young grass would sprout in
untended fields, insects crawl out towards
sunlight, and wild flowers cascade over
hills in coloured sheets, glistening

with nectar. They knew coarse undergrowth
would swell to creep across woodland,
becoming thicket and tangled wilderness,
giving cool brambled shade to their young.
In the last days, a great wind sprang up,
to bring the birds their promised liberation.

Vuyelwa Carlin
Birdsong

Cheep, wuckoo, chirrup: old, old pipings:
they pull, push, at our tongues, throats –

we strive for little crude sound-sculptures.
The perfection of cold chants: not heartless –

heartless is neither here nor there: they are other
as trees, green stalks – what music unheard

in those green, woody pipes?
They call and call – not for us. We love them:

it's nothing to them. The same phrase over and over,
we say – pressing them, little air-bones,

into shapes of Thought: but there's no holding them,
first harmonists; note-catcher.

⋆

Malleus, incus, stapes – latecomers,
last-minute developments, instruments of theory:

we chase music, make it conscious.
The first fliers, flapping leathers,

called harshly – if they called at all:
then the whittling down, hollowing out, warming up;

the feathering, the carving of horn: given back,
the whistles of wind, water, in stony, earthy channels.

GWYNETH LEWIS
Birds

Songs are sparking
from the beaks of birds – their work,
from the gentle dove to the hawk,

is to spread the words of their kind like seed
and grow them, a bush of sound and song,
the ground and confine of passion,

a home that matches power of voice,
an old round's unromantic place.
The curlew and willow warbler's songs

aren't ditties but threats of violence.
Forget the redbreast's lyricism,
this melody's forged with the beak's lance

and it's sharp. He's no philosopher,
the starling, but wild adulterer.
And the thrush is murderer.

GWYN THOMAS
Birds

Life has been plucked out of them and the bare white of death hangs on the long-blind, crucified bodies that are suspended with their heads in grapples of iron; on the heaps of their own blood they are as if stretching their necks in a mournful mute crowing; the heaviness of death is taut in them, it runs along the muscle, it is long in the vein:– birds on conveyors in a food factory.

We roast innocence in a furnace, lick our lips in the meat of suffering, we eat and gulp violent death and belch above the slaughtered remains. This is our holy communion.

John Davies

How To Make A Bird

Quick. A squirrel
launching the glider of its tail
flies up a trunk.

I watch what my hands
make of bandsawn wood.
Not much usually
though hands don't know that,
and anyway even our apple tree
flares only once a year.
Twisting, it can't untie its knot.

But it gives rise to birds, gives rise.
Carved birds too want to live,
blocked wings become wing blur,
heads turn to their shadows.
How to grasp what flies?

Catch, say, the dark star trilling
before it is a skylark.

R.S. Thomas

Bird Watching

Choosing amid many whisperings
the enamel platitudes
of the Mediterranean; Sappho
and Propertius at it
to impinge on the Telegraph's
stop press; to observe birds,
their wavering italics
in competition with the ocean's

serene gaze. The post chaise
was a necessary adjunct
of the grand tour; we thumb
our way, our arrival
as unsuspected as an occurrence
of influenza. A thousand
binoculars winnow
the thin haze. Eyes,
that in other places,
would be penetrating
the young women's amorphous
clothing can here notice
the lack of cosmetics
that distinguishes one warbler
from another. Winged God
approve that in a world
that has appropriated flight
to itself there are still people
like us, who believe
in the ability of the heart
to migrate momentarily between
the quotidian and the sublime.

John Barnie

How To Watch Birds

Shallows of the sea frozen over in sheets,
Crackling panes of ice that split, squeaked under foot,
And in between, wrinkled sand like buried ribs.
The tide was turning, sneaking in under the ice,
Cold runs of water like the clearest crystal.
We walked on the sand, wavered, slid, on the creaking sea,
And a steely wind tortured tears from our eyes,
So the world wobbled, flashed ripple-light
Off water and ice, while the cold dug deep
Into our bones, and the wind hammered our skulls.

Doug had brought brandy which we drained in large gulps,
And the glow-coloured liquid left us no warmer.
We were defeated. But the great black-backed gulls,
Redshanks and shelducks and barrel-chested geese
Stayed on, foursquare on ice or seafrozen stones,
Staring into the wind. We lurched, lunged back
to the road.
My head banged with pain
The cap of bone too cold
To touch, the wrinkled brain
Hunched in its hole like a toad.

Eiluned Lewis
Never Such a Place for Birds

There was never such a place for birds. With the turn of the year the ploughed fields were white with gulls that bred near one of the mountain lakes; early in April the curlews came inland with their desolate cry which Delia's quick ears were always the first to catch, and the rooks clamoured and argued over their nests, breaking off twigs from the trees with a side-ways wrench of their strong beaks, and walking mincingly on the lawn as they searched for moss.

Every year the house-martins built their nests outside Delia's and Lucy's bedroom window, and the drenched spring fields, where pools of rain-water winked with a thousand eyes, were full of tumbling, calling peewits. The pretty nut-hatches ran up and down the tree-trunks and the woodpeckers' rat-tat-tat echoed all day. They with their hammer and the great tits with their harsh sawing were as noisy as a carpenter's shop.

Along the river bank there were moor-hens, always engaged on some bustling business of their own, graceful dippers and water-wagtails and the brilliant, shy kingfishers, while sometimes a heron stood pensively fishing, or winged his sulky flight to the remote and reedy haunts of the wild duck.

One morning something woke Lucy very early before it was quite light. While she lay still in bed one small, sleepy bird piped a note, another answered, and thereupon there burst out such a clamour of voices, such an urgency of song that this seemed to be no ordinary daybreak, but one made above all others for gladness and rejoicing.

J.D. MALLINSON

Bird-Watching In Wales

(for Cedric Hayes, J.P.)

At last extent of Pembrokeshire
the clinging path holds its breath
against the lip of sheer cliffs
shoring up Saint David's Head;
in the gorse and matted beds
stonechat linger, linnets spin.

The half-island's tropic walk
descends from Penmaen Burrows
to bays lapping the south Gower;
sea air lures the yellowhammer,
hones the solo flight of crows,
draws the dunnet to the hedge.

Climbing into depths of sky
above the high, lonely valleys
of the Cambrian Mountains –
by Mynnydd Eppynt – buzzard
and the fork-tailed kite
hover at a rending height.

On reaches of the River Dee
down to Llangollen, dippers dip
and swallows dart beneath
stone arches of the bridge;
feinting, too, against the drift
wagtail perches, lightly lifts.

Francis Sackett
A Dream Of Birds

'I dreamt of birds,' she said,
Still in the grip of the tarantula's web.
We'd brought her from Gatwick,
Through English borders, I
Stopped in a Cotswold village.

She spoke of home in the East,
Reminded us of ghostly forests
Where lichen spread like warts,
'And now strange mushrooms grow'
She said, 'so huge, mysterious.'

'I had a dream...'
We'd caught her watching from the car
The languid flight of birds,
The pastel sky that smoothed to chocolate soil,
The way the trees were flighty, individual.

And then her shock –
Stock still she stood
As fruit cascaded from a shop-front
In garish green and orange,
Promiscuous row on row.

Then flowing with the fruit
Her tears, releasing strand
By strand the weakening web.
Her voice now lifting, soaring,
'I dreamt of birds,' she said.

JOHN POWELL WARD

Dreaming Birds

The eyes and feathers intermesh.
Descartes said birds were small machines.
A startled starling clattered off
And flew away at that, it screeched
That birds are loops in modern minds,
Weird flights, a mode, a fatal curve
Of values in the air. The thrush

Is proto-sculpture on the lawn,
The SS crow patrolling down
A motorway's hard shoulder struts
At sentry duty. From a pole
A blackbird soloist transmits
Its live performance and the cool
Woods pay to hear him, dark guitars

Are slung there and electric cries
Flash down the alleyways of spruce,
Afforestation's gentlest crop.
The dreamer Kant thought of a dove
That found air fretful and conceived
A purer flight in empty space.
I dream of swifts and soar asleep.

ROBERT GIBBINGS

Looking At The Wing

Have you ever *really* looked at a bird's wing? Have you ever thought of the difference between the short broad wings of birds that inhabit the woods and hedgerows, and the long tapering wings of those who live in the open. The green woodpecker, the jay, and the pheasant dodging through thick cover need something different to the wide-soaring gulls or the zenith-seeking swallows. The wings of a greenfinch are almost as broad as they are long, the average width of a swift's wing is scarcely a quarter of its length. The greenfinch's wing is gently cambered, and its fore-edge is nearly straight; the swift's wing is flat and curved like a scimitar.

And, apart from the manifold shapes, there is the indescribable subtlety of colouring, patches blending with each other to make bars across the forms, light and dark accents pencilling the margin of each feather.

Eifion Wyn

Birds At Evening

It was two birds at night-fall
 Were o'er the earth flying,
And the one to the other
 Was calling and crying–
  O but love the world over
   With all things doth mingle;
  And there's no bird that flieth
   But grieves to fly single.

It was two birds together
 As night was a-falling,
And the one to the other
 Was crying and calling–
  O there's love in all living
   If only one knew it;
  And each bird that is mateless
   With sorrow must rue it.

R.S. THOMAS

A Species

It is a crackling of song's twigs,
but dry like the brittle
but bitter laughter of a young girl
at a tart joke; the scratching
of a match on a bare hearth,
an attempt to get April going
before February has departed.
It is a symbol of our condition,
a species parochial and important,
erecting our small edifices
in the context of space-time,
domesticating the wildernesses
that geology has bequeathed us.
Its nest is a twigged hovel,
illuminated by jewels.
Those blue caskets exhibit, when opened,
the contents that are their programme.
Their phrases, such as they are,
were not listened to by emperor or clown.
It is free will that is our problem.
In the absence of such wings
as were denied us we insist
on inheriting others from the machine.
The eggs that we incubate bring forth
in addition to saints monsters,
the featherless brood whose one thing
in common with dunnocks is
that they do not migrate. We are fascinated
by evil; almost you could say
it is the plumage we acquire
by natural selection. There is a contradiction
here. Generally subdued feathers
in birds are compensated for
by luxuriant song. Not so these

whose frayed notes go with their plain clothes.
It is we who, gaudy as jays,
make cacophonous music under an egg-shell sky.

Gwilym R. Jones

Psalm To The Creatures

Let us celebrate the single-cloaked beings
Content in their coats of fur and feathers,
And the swimmers who wish no other garb than their skins.

Let us sing
The ants who do not reckon their hours of diligence
On their hillock-years
Because a forest of heather-bells
Sweetens their labour;
The common newt who is wiser than men,
And the woolly-bear who zig-zags on cabbage wine.

Let us envy
The cormorant who bathes in the precious colours
Of sunset on the sea;
The salmon, sunny his bliss,
Who knows how to breed young without charity;
The moon-drunk owl
Proud because night is the other side of day,
And the squirrel who slinks to Annwfn
To doze away the long barren season.

Let us weave praise
For the birds of legends,
Noah's dove and Branwen's starling
Who carried the mail across the waters,
And Rhiannon's birds
Who gave merry nights to the dead
And caused bones to dance.

And let us not forget
The hopping gander
Who gave a few quills to Bishop Morgan,
Giving the haven of its wings to the Welsh language,
And the mother-hens who provided
Welsh beds with their warmth.

GWYNETH LEWIS
Woods

Midwinter and this beech wood's mind
is somewhere else. Like fallen light

snow's broken glass fills up the furrows.
Nothing that doesn't have to moves.

We walk through a frozen waterfall
of boles, all held in vertical

except for the careful woodpile laid
In pencils across a tidied glade.

Look back and from the place we were
a bird calls out because we're not there,

a double note whose range expands,
pushing the line where our racket ends

out ever further. That elaborate song
can only exist because we're gone.

A vandal, I shatter that place with a stone.
The bird is for silence. I am for home.

Francis Kilvert
The Bird Church

Diary, 1870
I went into the churchyard under the feathering larch which sweeps over the gate. The ivy-grown old church with its noble tower stood beautiful and silent amongst the elms with its graves at its feet. Everything was still. No one was about or moving and the only sound was the singing of birds. The place was all in a charm of singing, full of peace and quiet sunshine. It seemed to be given up to the birds and their morning hymns. It was the birdchurch, the church among the birds.

Euros Bowen
Winged In Gold

The bird swerved dapple-white in the blue sky, paused, and then swam into the commotion of rays between the sun and the lake.

The sleek wings vibrating in the still air stirred a venture in the heart, and yielding to the brightness, every fear fled with the wonder of the flight.

But the bird began to falter in the flame, and then slipped and fell into the fire on the water below, and all the feathers were burned in the intense ferment.

Blinded by the light, the soul followed the thrill, the sparkle drawing it into the embracing brightness, until all the senses fell into the shimmering fire.

The imagination, as it watched, weakened with discontent the mind adding faults to regrets at the sight of body and wings perishing like dross in the embers.

Then with a sudden turn, out of the scattered ashes the bird rose high, all winged in purified gold.

R.S. Thomas

Sea-watching

Grey waters, vast
as an area of prayer
that one enters. Daily
over a period of years
I have let the eye rest on them.
Was I waiting for something?
Nothing
but that continuous waving
that is without meaning
occurred.
Ah, but a rare bird is
rare. It is when one is not looking,
at times one is not there
that it comes.
You must wear your eyes out.
as others their knees.
I became the hermit
of the rocks, habited with the wind
and the mist. There were days,
so beautiful the emptiness
it might have filled,
its absence
was as its presence; not to be told
any more, so single my mind
after its long fast,
my watching from praying.

R.S. Thomas

A Crown

...towards the end of the month the birds of prey come by. Last year in August I saw a long-eared owl sitting on a branch in the lane to Ty'n Parc; and this year Menna saw one in the lane to Bodwyddog. This is also the time to keep your eyes open for the harriers, the hen harrier and the marsh harrier and even the osprey if you're lucky. So, having been to the Eistedfodd, don't think that there isn't a crown for you, too somewhere in the world of nature.

R.S. Thomas

Inextinguishable

Birds have started to sing. The song thrush is at it from to time, and the goldcrest. Nature can't wait, even though there are rough times between us and the spring. I remember how in the dark days of the war, a bluetit started singing one January, raising our spirits. Life is stronger than death. Even though it appears otherwise very often, life, like love itself, gives the impression that it is inextinguishabable, and even if they were both to die out on earth, there are other places where they would continue to flower.

Cyphers

Strange birds we had
never seen, a portent
of some final freeze set
to grip the world

Vuyelwa Carlin

Icarus

– Beached salty barbs, salt-white;
long supples
from swifts' tails;

and after moonlight,
when nightingales
richly, moltenly called and called,

I gathered thorn-caught down,
built song
into these undersides!

I tied the quills with thin
strong silk: the mesh
– complex, patterned with utmost

delicate-fingered pride –
of little curls,
– this was wax-held.

He fetched and carried
– brought bread, crimson seeds:
and as I plaited,

arranged the threads
for turning the feathers sideways
for the wings' rise,

I spoke to him – my dark
reluctant boy –
warned him! Stranger,

as young things are,
he kicked the water-pitcher: barely
bent his soft ear.

R.S. Thomas

Miraculous Lives

For many centuries man yearned to fly, and at last he succeeded. But long before we appeared on earth the birds had mastered the feat with less tumult and fuss, and without taxing the resources of their environment, or using this ability to destroy their own kind. So birds are part of the wonder of April, causing us to ponder deeply their miraculous lives. But to appreciate them fully one must be very alert, because several of them only pop into Llŷn on their way northwards. I used to think there were not more than fifty different different types of bird nesting in the parish at Aberdaron; and yet while I was living there, by keeping my eyes open at the right times, I saw around a hundred and eighty species.

T. E. Nicholas

To A Sparrow

(Swansea Prison, 1940)

Look, here's another bread-crumb for your piping,
And a piece of apple as a sweetener .
It gladdens me to hear your steady pecking;
It's good to see your cloak of grey once more,
You've travelled here, perhaps, from Pembroke's reaches,
From the gorse and heather on Y Frenni's height,
And maybe on grey wing you've trilled your measures
Above fair Ceredigion at dawn's first light.
Accept the bread: had I a drop of wine
Pressed from a distant country's sweet grape-cluster,
We two could take, amid war's turbulence,
Communion, though the cell lacks cross and altar.
The bread's as holy as it needs to be,
Offering of a heart not under lock and key.

GLENDA BEAGAN
The Last Thrush

Each evening the thrush would come. She would hear its click and thump, that sharp repeated sound, that hammer on the anvil. She could not see it. Lying here, how could she? But it was almost as if she could. See it. Be it. Be which of them though? There are two of them out there. Thrush and snail. And the air is warm and calm as the sound carries. It fills the room.

'Time for your medication, Mrs. Shone. Can you manage dear? Let me help you sit up. That's it...'

Her voice is too tired to move in the air that holds the sound of the thrush on the step. There it is again. Across the garden at the far end by the shed. The sound has travelled a long way to climb through the white window. And why should such a sound be comforting? It is a murderous sound. And yet there is a closeness to it. A familiar shape.

CLICK. Click. Click. Click. THUMP.

And the probing bill of the thrush scoops thickly, scoops thinly in the softness inside the shell.

Her own pain is misted but still there somehow. Constantly there in the background. Like water seeping slowly on a stone. Out there in the garden on the step of the shed the thrush declares itself. The Russian vine that half buries the shed shift lightly like an animal in its sleep and moves its cream white flowers.

Dr. Whittaker called today. She smiled at him and the effort of the smile creased and set on her face. Is this what a death mask is? Is this what it means? How fond of him. She has grown so fond of him over the years. They are the same age. Yes, exactly. He'd just joined old Dr. Garnett's practice when she was expecting Stephen. Does he ever think about Stephen? Does he ever wonder what he might have been?

And when he asked her whether she felt she needed more of the painkiller, she found, for once, that her voice could be clean and strong. It was her voice. Her own. And she was proud, not so much of the words, their meaning, though that was important too, but of their clarity, their sureness. She was still here.

'No,' she said, pulling the words up from a cool place she still kept inside her. 'No. Really.' And the smile was stuck on her face though she wanted to move it. I don't need any more. I'm floating about as it is. As if I'm not properly here. As it is.'

He had smiled then, touched her lightly on the arm. And he was such a big man, clumsy really, though for all his awkwardness his touch was so *bright.* And she has wanted to thank him for the deep space he made in the room. A space for breathing. How did he feel about this, about her? They had grown old together, hadn't they? Isn't it strange? And yet they were neither of them old. Not *old.* Not really. She was a long way off growing *really* old. But what did growing old have to do with dying? With this?

Dr. Whittaker moved softly in the room. She saw him write the prescription. She saw him hand it to the nurse. She heard the click of his bag as it closed. And the click of that bag, so near, was somehow so much further away than that other click, that thump on the step outside. It was ridiculous. How could she possibly know what it was like, how it felt, to be a snail being slowly eaten by a thrush?

But she did know. She felt it. Perhaps God was like a thrush? Hammering. Pounding. Probing inside the human shell. Did she believe in God? Did she believe there was anything out there? In the end?

ANNA WIGLEY

Duck-shooting

That was the summer you took me
on gunmetal mornings, early,
to strange deserted places:

wet ground, forests of rushes,
hard grass stubbling
from a sodden mattress.

Mindful of my privilege
I was silent as instructed,
trod softly in the wake

of your long legs and galoshes.
In the holster of your hip
the butt of your rifle jogged.

Toads the colour of mud
panted silently on mud ledges.
We caught the electric trace

of a snake. No wind.
Just a cold smell of water
and the sky getting lower.

On a jigsaw of cracked sludge
you crooked a knee,
patted me down, slid the catch;

I saw nothing but the back of your head
as you leaned like a cat
into the eye of the sight,

clenching yourself round the gun
until you had it tamed,
and with a slow squeeze let death out.

The ducks were soft and loose
as bundles of silk.
Their rainbowed necks

lolled from the mouth of your bag.
Later we would pick the shot
from the stopped hearts

be soldierly and not mind
the sick tug of quills from flesh,
the high bier of feathers.

Leslie Norris
The Mallard

A duck can't look at you directly, since their eyes are set at the sides of their heads, so they turn to look at you with one beady eye. This gives them a comically knowing expression. When she'd see there was no more food she'd race over the lawn and plunge into the water, throwing it ecstatically over her back and head as she rocked vigorously backward and forward. Then she'd squawk once or twice, swim up the stream, and take off. I'd see her circle the house, her neck outstretched, her hammerhead set at an angle.

"Bill bill bill!" I'd call, and she'd give one raucous answer before flying swiftly off, her stubby wings flashing.

In the warm afternoons the young drakes come over and sit on the lawn or indulge in loud splashing horseplay in the water. They are incredibly handsome in their breeding plumage, reminding me of groups of very young men dressed in their finery, parading for no other purpose than the gallant manipulation of their fashionable clothes. My friends and I were rather like this, when we were sixteen or seventeen...

Last Tuesday my dark mallard duck didn't come to be fed as usual. I got up early just the same. There had been some shooting the night before in the fields behind the house, but I hadn't taken much notice of it. Rasbridge's boy after pigeons I thought. I got the car out when it became obvious my duck wasn't hungry, and drove through the early lanes on the downs.

Just before lunch, about eleven o'clock I suppose, I went down to the end of my paddock and found the duck. She was dead. She had been shot through the breast and she was dead and stiff. I picked her up. She was unbelievably light and her poor feathers were dry and harsh. Her eye was a blob of excrement. That morning I had seen in one of the lanes the body of a hare which had been knocked by a car. A crow was standing on it, tearing at the soft belly. I had accepted this as one of the things that happened, but I was shaking angry as I brought the duck home. I buried her in the garden, knowing how useless it was.

I had a bad night that night, unusual for me, and I didn't sleep much until morning. When I got up I didn't want breakfast, so I went into the garden. The baker's van was down the road a little way. He was probably delivering to Mrs. Rogers. I walked down the drive and leaned on the gate. Rasbridge drove up in his green estate car. When he saw me, he pulled up and leapt out.

"A pleasant day, Simmonds," he said.

I opened the gate and walked toward him

"Things are beginning to move," he said. "I've just been over to see my wheat and it looks good, really good."

He looked over the gate at my roses.

"By jove," he said, "your garden is looking very well too."

He smiled at me as if the sun shone for him alone.

"By the way," he said, "I've had to cull some of the mallards. Far too many of them, you know – they're keeping me poor."

I don't know what I said, but he stopped laughing and swung at me. It was pitiable really. I'd hit him twice before his fist had finished its back swing, and a slow trickle of blood came from his nose. Then suddenly I was crouching and weaving, my left hooking him to head and body so hard I thought he'd snap. Whatever it was I had thought buried in me was not dead. There was no need for the right hand I gave him as he went down. I would have stamped on him, I think, if the baker hadn't grabbed me. Strangely enough I wasn't upset. I looked down at Rasbridge, at his yellow face with the quick swelling on the temple above his right eyebrow, the bruise on the cheekbone and the right side of his jaw. I suppose I must have hit him seventeen or eighteen times.

GILLIAN CLARKE
Wild Sound

A day of birds:
at dawn, my car abandoned,
engine humming at the junction.
I'm stopping the traffic, one hand up
against the hot breath of a lorry.
The other lifts the weightless silk of a swift
like a beating heart from the road.
I throw it to the wind
above the lorry and the eaves
where sky begins.

Then, in a brown underground corridor at the BBC,
an eagle owl in a hurry:
'Can't stop. On its way to Moscow.'
Then it's gone, an absence
in a wilderness,
its talons' hooked steel,
its eye planetary.

Hours later I'm still breathing
the musk of feathers. Surely
the listeners to the radio
could sense, between the words,
wild sound, hot, quivering, alive,
a wingbeat on the footless air,
a stare of gold.

Aled Vaughan
The White Dove

...a white dove came curving swiftly and silently out of the black clouds. It made three smooth circles round the stackyard and then, with a little flutter, it settled on the high rib of our barn roof.

I was transformed. I was no longer myself, a boy with two arms, two legs, and a face. I was the earth, everyone, everywhere, and I drifted silently around the barn, my eyes always on the white dove. It stood delicately on the roof, carved in snowflakes, a dazzling light that made a joke of the sombre world. Its small unblemished breast rose and fell evenly in confident challenge to the threatening sky. Time had gone, and was standing in the centre of eternity.

A howling gust of wind rode menacingly across the black and grey countryside. It struck cruelly at the side of the dove. The white form lost its grace; wings screamed, and feathers were chaotic with fright. My omniscience shrivelled: I was aware again of the sombreness of the afternoon.

The bird regained its dazzling beauty, but my peace was destroyed. Time was back, pressing callously. I was now full of a tumbling desire to hold the dove safely in my hands. Before peace could return I would have to possess it, to protect it, to have it with me always. I ran to the cart shed, and my eagerness gave me strength to carry the long ladder which I placed against the barn wall. When I reached the roof the dove was still there, almost within reach. My joy was back; but not calm and strong as before. I climbed higher to balance precariously on the top stave, my knees pressed against the hard tile coping of the roof. But I was beyond the vicious hand of danger: the dove had exterminated it. Making endearing noises my tongue had never discovered before I pushed my hand along the cold slates. The bird turned its head, and examined my crawling fingers with round flat eyes the colour of new pennies. And then, just as I was about to touch it, it fluttered gently, swooped above the sloping roof, and flew straight through the open doorway of the cart shed. I clutched at the slates. They had suddenly become the jagged teeth of danger grinning at me. I descended the ladder with painful care.

In the enclosed shed the dove had perched itself on a higher rafter, and as I closed the giant doors to trap it I knew I was bordering on evil.

With ancient cunning I examined every possible way of reaching the bird. But it was way up beyond anything I could climb, and I knew the ladder was too long to stand upright in the shed. Then the evil gripped me completely, and I relished it. Outside, after making sure that no one was looking, I helped myself to a pocketful of stones. I returned, fastened the doors, and took aim. The first stone missed. It exploded against the galvanized roof, and the dove inclined its head towards the noise, asking a silent question. But the second stone struck home and my prey threw itself helplessly against its harsh prison wall. I was jubilant. But there was something terrifying about the way the bird had not uttered a sound when the stone violated it. I struck again, and in a hysterical attempt to escape the dove crashed into a steel girder. As it fell into my waiting arms its wings thrashed ecstatically.

And oh, the searing joy of holding it, of feeling its softly curving feather-covered body filling the hollows of my hands! Its heart ticked sharply against my palms as if the life in it were thrusting itself forward to communicate and immerse itself in mine. And it succeeded in its quest, for at that moment I was as one with the dove; a white flash of happiness, free to fly over the cumbersome world or to explore the smooth sky. The evil had never been. 'Oh my lovely, lovely, lovely dove!' I crooned. 'My beautiful white dove!'

I carried it out of the prison. The moment it saw the sky and fields it tried to escape. It struggled in my hands and its startled eyes blinked with alarm. I shrank with unhappiness. It didn't want me, didn't understand me. 'I won't hurt you!' I sobbed, holding it directly in front of me so that it could understand the look on my face. 'I won't hurt you! I'll be your greatest friend! I'll spend every evening and all Saturday and Sunday feeding you!'

It struggled again, and I had to hold it firmly. Everything was confused because I didn't want to force it to do anything against its will, and yet I wanted to keep it. After it had settled and I was thinking it had understood I wanted to be its friend, its beak opened and a small ball of blood rolled off its creamy tongue and broke on the back of my hand. Stunned, I watched it trickling warmly down to my wrist: Then came a terrible remorse. 'Forgive me! Forgive me!' I cried, holding its warm body firmly to my breast. 'I didn't mean to hurt you! I only wanted to be your friend! Will you forgive me? Am I forgiven?' I held it away from me and opened my hands, hoping that if I were to offer it its freedom my crime would be redeemed, and that if it didn't fly away it would be proof that it had forgiven me. But my fingers had scarcely broken away from the feathers when the wings opened and without a sound its white form streaked through the air and climbed towards the black clouds. It vanished. The world was now an endless cave and I was alone, lost, as lonely as the sea on a stormy night. My heart could hold no more and I wept as I ran towards the grey house.

Gwenallt Jones
Pigeons

The workers tended their pigeons in the evening,
On the Hill, after the day's servitude,
Each coop with its platform at the top of the garden
Releasing its white cloud.

They were sent to North Wales and to England,
Loosed from the baskets to the sky,
But returned from the heart of distant beauty
To our South's neighbourly poverty.

They would circle about in the smoke-filled sky
Giving colour to the twisted gloom;
Lumps of beauty in the midst of the haze;
The Holy Ghost's image above the Cwm.

The Holy Ghost sanctifying the smoke,
Turning worker to person of flesh and blood,
The cash nexus transformed in the order of grace
And the Unions part of the household of God.

CHRISTOPHER MEREDITH
Griffri

Non warned us that the trees on the border side were full of spirits and she never went into them, not even into the fringe for a piss, though it meant she had to walk three bowshots to some other place. But we'd already peopled the trees with our own fears. Any heavy noise in a bramble was an enemy. Every scuffling was a ghost. Cadi thought that Eneas's soul could have gone into a bird, like Lleu in the story.

'See' he said, 'with all those branches it'd be easy for his soul to get tangled somewhere on its way up.'

We looked at one another wide eyed.

'In fact' he said, and I knew that he was going to speak my thoughts, 'he could have gone into a tree.'

We looked at the trees again. They were leafless by this time and the twigs clickclicked against one another in a stir of wind. There was a grove of immense beech trees nearby. There had been no beech trees at my old home and these, when I'd first seen them, had astonished me. The trunk of the largest of them now became shaped and fleshy as a man's back. Horrified and fascinated we walked around it. Looking up to where the branches started, I saw countless fragments of people – noses, cheeks, and especially bare heels, blending one greygreen part into the next. As we moved I looked at the trunk again and I felt that I was always seeing the back of someone who slowly kept turning away.

There was a high scream. Cadi ran past me very fast, making obscure noises like someone trying to be sick. I copied this action quite accurately without bothering to look in the direction he'd run from and I drew level with him as we reached the clearing. Cadi slowed as he ran out of breath and fear at the same time. We slid on the wet ground and fell together. I was ready to scramble up and run again but Cadi pulled at my shirt.

'The owl' he said. 'I saw him.'

'I didn't see the owl.'

'He went right over my head. Missed me by a hand breadth.'

I looked back into the trees and then down at my foster brother. His skin was whiter than his teeth.

'I didn't see him.'

I helped him up.

'A corpse bird' he said. 'Worse if you didn't.'

I shrugged. 'There's always owls.'

As our terror ebbed further Cadi's breath came back and with it excitement. We debated whether a man's soul could go into a tree or bird. Cadi was quiet sometimes and I knew he was thinking about the owl so I kept talking. At first we thought the bird was plausible but the tree wasn't, because birds like people have limbs and eyes and can move. But then we thought of Christ in the bread and wine and the evidence of the strange tree, and we were unsure.

We decided to appeal to Non on the matter, as she had more patience with us than Gwrgant concerning such things. It took a long time before we could make our story and the drift of our thinking clear to her, mainly because we both spoke at once and used a lot of pronouns without saying what they referred to until she cross examined us.

She put her hand on Cadi's forehead and watched him while he talked.

'An owl?' she said.

'So can men's souls go into these things?' I said.

'No' she said with great sureness, smiling as if the question was silly, and she looked uncertainly towards the trees.

IDRIS DAVIES

Send Out Your Homing Pigeons, Dai

Send out your homing pigeons, Dai,
Your blue-grey pigeons, hard as nails,
Send them with messages tied to their wings,
Words of your anger, words of your love.
Send them to Dover, to Glasgow, to Cork,
Send them to the wharves of Hull and of Belfast,
To the harbours of Liverpool and Dublin and Leith,
Send them to the islands and out of the oceans,
To the wild wet islands of the northen sea
Where little grey women go out in heavy shawls

At the hour of dusk to gaze on the merciless waters,
And send them to the decorated islands of the south
Where the mineowner and his tall stiff lady
Walk round and round the rose-pink hotel, day after
day after day.
Send out your pigeons, Dai, send them out
With words of your anger and your love and your
pride,
With stern little sentences wrought in your heart,
Send out your pigeons, flashing and dazzling towards
the sun.
Go out, pigeons bach, and do what Dai tells you.

BRENDA CHAMBERLAIN

Tide-race

We had come with infinite caution down the precipitous holdless grass of the mountainside. Never before on any hill have I known such sheer grass. To slip a few inches, to lose the slightest control, would be enough to set a body rolling and bouncing over the cliffs into the waves. The wind was piercingly cold, so I had borrowed two of Stewart's sweaters and a pair of his old army trousers turned up in many folds, and a raincoat. By going barefoot, it was possible to move comfortably, digging heels and fingers into the turf. Below the awful expanse of grassy precipice came the ledges of firm and honest rock giving sound hold.

Our minds grew dazed by the thunder of the conflicting tides. As we let ourselves down the last yards where a few tussocks of thrift wait to crumble from the slope under unwary fingers, we came face to face with the Ancient Mariner. With bent knees and one hand against the rock he moved along a narrow lip made greasy with the droppings of birds. On his arm he carried a basket full of gulls' and razorbills' eggs bedded in fleece. Calmly plundering the hatcheries, with nothing but the assurance of balance to keep him from death, he moved warily and sinuously as a weasel. Swinging round with an extravagant gesture of alarm at sight of us above him, he nearly pitched forward over the rocks. He had been walking with his glass eye towards us. He was unshaven and his finger-nails were long, black, and hooked as talons.

Stewart called out harshly to him:

'This is a sanctuary for birds; you have no right to take so many eggs!'

For answer, he blew him a kiss, and touched an egg with his foot so that it rolled away over the edge of the precipice.

Deeply hurt, Stewart moved on, his cheeks and neck a deep red with mortification.

A hen and cock bird stood side by side, the mother bird sheltering her green egg between prehistoric feet. Having no nest in which to lay it, she guarded it against the soft wall of her belly. She cooed, nodded, danced, bowed, in reply to her mate. The cliffs murmured with their warm and mysterious communication. She was maternal and careless all at the same time. Feeling the need for a silver fish, she shuffled off the ledge, taking the egg with her.

'This stench is unbearable,' shouted Stewart. 'My God, how these birds do stink.'

Feeling like a pigmy, I climbed up and down among the crags. The sea was emerald, frothed with white. In lee of the land, submerged rocks of the reef showed as soft purple stains under the water.

We began to collect a few eggs while birds circled wildly round us. Herring gulls lay their eggs in shallow, primitive nests made of dead grass, feathers, sheeps' wool, or seaweed, along the rocky shore; or simply drop their eggs in depressions on the grass slopes. We found razorbills' eggs hidden in deep crannies. They were of a chalky white splashed with brown blotches the colour of old blood, and were more beautiful than the mottled dun-green eggs of the herring gull. Against the stones whitened with bird-droppings. They were perfectly camouflaged. Whenever we found a gull's nest with three eggs in it. Stewart broke one to test whether it was addled, for usually if the full clutch was there, it meant that the chicks had begun to form. When we had gathered about two dozen eggs for the making of omelettes, we hid them under a fleece ready to put into our bag on the way back to the west side.

Thomas Pennant

Plygan

Upon *Christmas* day, about three o'clock in the morning, most of the parishioners assembled in church, and after prayers and a sermon, continued there singing psalms and hymns with great devotion till broad day; and if, through age or infirmity, any were disabled from attending, they never failed having prayers at home, and carols on our SAVIOUR'S nativity. The former part of the custom is still preserved; but too often perverted into intemperance. This act of devotion is called *Plygan*, or the *Crowing of the Cock*. It has been a general belief among the superstitious, that instantly,

at his warning,
'Whether in sea or tire, in earth or air,
Th' extravagant and erring spirit hies
To his confine

But during the holy season, the Cock was supposed to exert his power throughout the night; from which, undoubtedly, originated the Welsh word *Plygan*, as applied to this custom. Accordingly, *Shakespeare* finely describes this old opinion:

Some say, that ever 'gainst that season comes
Wherein our SAVIOUR'S birth is celebrated,
The bird of dawning singeth all night long:
and then, they say, no spirit walks abroad:
The nights are wholesome: then no planets strike:
No fairy takes: no witch hath power to charm,
So hallowed and so gracious is the time.

Hilary Llewellyn-Williams

Hunting the Wren

The boys are out in the frost.
Redeyed pack in the black sticks

of the wood, crunching tracks,
shaking snow
from shoved-aside branches;
faces rubbed raw
poor boys
numb and raw with cold
purplish fingers grabbing.
They are coming this way
fists bright with holly
who run and tiptoe and follow
under a bloody sun:
Milder and Molder
and Jackie the Can
and Johnny Red Nose
and everyone.

They are coming this way
treading dead leaves
empty trees overhead.
They roll in laughter
but under their black jackets
they brandish
death;
their smiles hide
the lanterns, the hollow box,
the toothed snares.
They are after blood in the wood.
Shabby bandits
in the gathering dusk
drunk with good hunting
they come, they come.

Their burden is heavy
as they climb the slow hill
towards town,
the box all ribboned around
which they hold
turn and turn
about, as owls come out.

Rough boys with stony faces
now graced with heroes' eyes
in the twilight, in pride
of the deed done.

Hours spent scouring the hills
and the forest thorns
since morning crept over
slate roofs and ponds:
all for the sake of an old song
and dance, stories
of questing for dragons
the black boar
of old winter, tushed ice.
Only the best
beast of the wood
will do to die
till spring shines.
Away from good food and warm fires
they spent the day with monsters
fought over bushes and briars –
they struggled, they won.

The last rays of the brief day
follow the noisy crew
with their garland box
that rattles like a nut
with the fruit of all their daring:
a handful of feathers
a spoonful of blood.
Good luck
drink up
a new year has begun!

says Milder to Molder
says Jackie the Can
says Johnny Red Nose
says everyone.

Hunting the Wren
This custom, once widespread in the British Isles, involved young men killing a wren on St Stephen's Day (Boxing Day), putting the wren into a decorated box, and carrying it from house to house in return for pennies. The traditional song accompanying this custom is usually known as *The Cutty Wren*. One version begins:

"O where are you going?" says Milder to Molder.
"We're hunting the wren" says Jackie the Can.
"We're hunting the wren" says Johnnie Red Nose.
"We're hunting the wren" says everyone.

SILVAN EVANS
Bygones

Something similar to the 'hunting of the wren' was not unknown to the Principality as late as as about a century ago, or later. In the Christmas holidays it was the custom of a certain number of young men, not necessarily boys, to visit the abodes of such couples as had been married within the year. The order of the night – for it was strictly a nightly performance – was to this effect. Having caught a wren, they placed it on a miniature bier made for the occasion, and carried it in process on towards the house which they intended to visit. Having arrived they serenaded the master and mistress of the house under their bedroom window with the following doggerel;-

Dyma'r dryw,
Os yw e'n fyw,
Neu dderyn to
I gael ei rostio

That is:–

Here is the wren,
If he is alive,
Or a sparrow
To be roasted.

If they could not catch a wren for the occasion, it was lawful to substitute a sparrow. The husband, if agreeable, would then open the door, admit the party, and regale them with plenty of Christmas ale, the obtaining of which being the principal object of the whole performance.

THE MABINOGION

Branwen Daughter Of Llŷr

...she reared a starling on the end of her kneading-trough and taught it words and instructed the bird what manner of man her brother was. And she brought a letter of the woes and the dishonour that were upon her. And the letter was fastened under the root of the bird's wings and sent towards Wales. And the bird came to this Island. The place where it found Bendigeidfran was at Caer Seint in Arfon, at an assembly of his one day. And it alighted on his shoulder and ruffled its feathers so that the letter was seen and it was known that the bird had been reared among dwellings.

And then the letter was taken and examined. And when the letter was read he grieved to hear of the affliction that was upon Branwen.

EMYR HUMPHREYS

Branwen's Starling

1

The sun was on his side
    The wind set fair, the sea
A cradle that would break
    A fall, while tirelessly

That clown among the birds
    Flew looking for respect
And under his warm wing
    The painful letter kept.

That lesson that he learnt
    Before the kitchen fire,
Perched on the kneading trough,
    Now part of his attire.

The woman's fingers worked,
    Her face a sorrowing mask;
Her skillful stitching bound
    His body to his task.

Alas! those gentle hands
    That once were smooth and kissed,
Cramped and captive, scarred
    Like the two hands of Christ.

His burden is her woe,
    Her sighs must cross the sea
Under the starling's wing,
    A sister's misery.

2

That day he started out
    As swiftly as a glance,
Rising above the Tower,
    He had no second chance.

Was it the hour before dawn,
    With frost thick on the grass,
Or moonlight or the stars
    That saw it come to pass?

It must have been still dark
    The day he left her hands
Before the morning bell
    Awoke the warrior bands.

Before the chimney smoke
    Announced the fires lit,
And brought the butcher boy
    Yawning towards the gate.

Already like a stain
    Across the unchanging sky
He saw the only course
    Her tears would let him fly.

Let the cold sea stay green
    And motionless as glass,
And let his seed of song
    Grow in the wilderness.

Until the hermit sun
    Emerges to display
Peaks and pyramids,
    The monuments of day.

And, like a rousing shout
    After long silence, shine
The mountains into view,
    Cold water into wine.

3

Whatever time it took
    That journey from the earth
Into the nothingness
    Where myths are given birth,

The starling reached the land,
    He circled overhead
Where the shoreless seas
    Shrink to a river bed,

And searches among the throng
    Of figures in a field
For that one soul apart,
    A shoulder and a shield,

Like something sent from heaven
　　To make the mighty wise.
He took him in his court,
　　A giant for his prize.

One ruffle of his wing
　　Brought her note to light,
But he had words as well
　　To rehearse her plight,

How she was made to slave
　　Above the kitchen fire,
Torn from her husband's love,
　　Insulted in her bower.

Her sigh became his song,
　　She taught him words, her name,
The message that he bore,
　　That flight that earned his fame.

4
What happened to the bird
　　The legend does not tell
Did he return forthwith
　　To the sad woman's cell.

Or sink exhausted there
　　Unburdened, his abode
A grave upon the beach
　　That Brân kneeled to prepare,

Or did he join the ship
　　That led the vengeful fleet
Bound for the Irish shore,
　　And from the rigging call
Each warrior at his oar?

The mast his stage, he plies
 Unruly parodies
A blackbird in the sails
 With thrush's melodies

Their laughter never fails,
 Their smiles are bright like swords,
As though their world were free
 Of grief and tragedy.

Ron Berry

Hunters And Hunted

...Miskin crooked a finger at the landlord, who deceptively walked like a pansy. 'The crack-shot himself,' Wills said. 'How's everything up in the Gwynt level? Turn about, Jennie, there's a customer waiting.'

Jennie hurried down the bar. Miskin took nine pigeon rings from his pocket, rattled them in his hand, and allowed one to tamp on the counter. 'Wait, Tommy, don't get riled,' he said.

'If you've been shooting racing birds, I'll shop you for certain.'

'I'd be a mug.' Miskin opened his hand. 'Found them this afternoon, all nice and tidy scattered among enough feathers to stuff a pillow.'

'Bastarding hawk,' Wills said.

'Falcon, man, falcon. Lost any pigeons lately?'

'My Bordeau winner disappeared only last week.'

'Check these numbers.'

Wills scooped up the rings. 'Come down to the kitchen,' he said. 'Bring your beer.'

Mrs. Wills sat beside the fire, reading a magazine. She said, 'Hullo, there, you're quite a stranger,' and crossed her legs.

'Jennie needs help up in the bar,' ordered Wills.

She flounced past Miskin. 'No peace for the wicked. Tell my father I'm sorry I ever left Blaenddu,' she said vindictively.

'Sure thing,' Miskin promised.

Wills scrutinized the rings, placing them in a row on the table. 'Well, wella-good Christ, *here* it is. That hawk killed her.'

Miskin scratched his nose. 'Before making any suggestions, Tommy, remember it's illegal to shoot falcons.'

'Every time you've shown us a dead hawk you've had your couple of quid. Miskin, bring us this bastard and I'll arrange for our club members to give you one extra. Three, I'll guarantee you three quid.'

'Tommy, your racing birds are being knocked off by falcons, not hawks.' Miskin drank some beer. 'I want a fiver,'

'I'll shoot the bloody thing myself first. Where'd you find these rings?'

'At the bottom of the quarry, just above Blaenddu police station. If you're caught, Tommy, it'll cost you twenty-five quid. Just calculate,' Miskin added, taking his bony forehead nearer the landlord's face.

'Mr. Wi-ills!' sang out Jennie from overhead.

'Hark at her,' Wills muttered to himself.

Miskin spat noisily into the fire. 'There's a pair of falcons hanging around Blaenddu. If they nest in the quarry as they used to during the War, the pigeon club members are going to lose some valuable stock. Don't ask me to bring you a dead falcon once they've started nesting, 'cause I shan't. See ?'

'Wait here a few minutes,'

'Fetch me a pint, Tommy, if you don't mind.'

Will returned with two bottles. He poured one in Miskin's glass, drank direct out of the other. 'Tell you what I'll do. Show me these two falcons at our next meeting, and I'll guarantee you a fiver.'

'Nothing doing.'

'Why not?' demanded Wills, showing an ugly lip line.

'I'll shoot the cock or the hen, depends which one I line up. Most likely the other one will fly off somewhere after another mate.'

Wills took a quick sup from his bottle. 'Blaenddu is three miles from Tosteg. Why don't you approach some of the fanciers up your way?'

'They're all members of your club, Tommy. In any case, you won't find falcons *except* in Blaenddu. It's the only place they'll get any peace. Three miles, Tommy! What's three miles to a bird that can shift at two hundred miles a bloody hour?'

Gillian Clarke
Mass Of The Birds

Frances, this morning,
buttercup dust on our sandals,
we drift back from early walks,
bring roses in long briars,
foxglove, bedstraw, meadowsweet,
cow parsley, ragged robin.

The mist is off the fields. Swifts
spin their shrill litanies.
Under the barn's beaten silver
incense of cut grass, creosote,
the sun's mat at the door.
We bring our privacies.

Rough table. Circle of chairs.
A heel of granary loaf.
Wine over from last night's supper.
A leather book. Luke. Romans.
Corinthians. Silences.
A congregation of eight.

The lapsed, the doubting, those
here for the first time, others
regular at named churches
share the meaning of breaking bread,
of sipping from one glass,
of naming you.

Mass of the birds. A blackbird calls,
a wren responds, calling, answering
what we can only feel.
We offer this as the sun
raises its wafer too brilliant
to look at or understand.

Do you remember the elder
that was sick to death last year,
all skin and bone in the arms
of a rambling rose? This year
it flourishes, grows green,
supports the rose.

MENNA ELFYN

A Bird In Hand

If you ask,
what's this muse?

A child finds
at the bottom of the school yard
one broad March morning
a small bird
hurt.
Goes to it gently, fondling it. Makes a nest
of her ready hands.
Its beak begs life
between two thumbs.

Again, if you ask
what's the Welsh muse?

The littlest of birds,
a wren, unobserved
in a dark wood.
It squats in an infected elm,
makes merry, does not die.

And if the men of the muse
ask, how is it being a women poet?
I'll show them wings
in a free, Decemberless sky –

to prefigure on a page of heaven
generosity above the Earth,
before returning
to feed
a stepful of sparrows
at the door, and tremble.

LESLIE NORRIS
A Flight Of Geese

'I had a cousin in Cardiganshire who was an expert with geese,' my uncle said after a silence. 'Kept all the varieties in his time. People used to come from all over the country to buy breeding stock from him. Oh, what a sight to see his flocks on the moors – great flocks of geese, marching like Prussians! He used to clip their wings at the elbow so they couldn't fly, and then, once they were old enough, out they'd go on the open moors, white geese, grey geese. They never strayed. At dusk they'd come high-stepping into his yard and the whole mountain would be full of their voices. I often stayed with him when I was young.

'He sent us a goose every year – two geese: one for Michaelmas and another for Christmas, always trussed and ready for cooking. He used to send them by bus – a bewildering journey, with many changes – but none of them ever failed to reach us. I used to wait here, on the square, for the bus to come in from Brecon toward late afternoon. The conductor would hand me a large hamper with our goose inside, and I'd stagger home with it. We used to cook it on a spit, rotating it in front of a blaze of a fire, a pan beneath to catch the melting fat. We took turns at basting it as it spun slowly – first one way, then the other – so that it wouldn't burn. Every Michaelmas, and every Christmas for years. What feasts we had then! Nor was that the end of the goose's usefulness. After the cooking we put the solidified goose grease in jars and kept it as a cure for sore throats and chest colds and bronchitis. I can remember my mother rubbing it on my bare chest and throat when I was a small boy. I can remember its gross smell, the thick feel of the grease on my skin. I hated that, although the old people swore by it as a curative.

'And even the bed I slept on owed its comfort to my cousin's geese, for the bed was stuffed with feathers from his birds. My mother made a huge envelope of blue and white striped ticking and filled it with goose feathers, making the whole thing plump and soft as a cloud. We all sleep well when we're young, but nobody could have slept softer and deeper than I did in my goose-feathered bed.'

My uncle held out his hand in front of him. 'You see this hand?' he asked. 'The hand is a superb instrument. This hand of mine can do all manner of things: it can wield a hammer, pick up a pin, it can point a chisel to the exact splitting place of a stone, it can create, it can destroy. My cousin's hands were to do with geese. He had huge hands. Here, on the inside of his thumb and forefinger, he had long callouses, incredibly hard, from feathering geese. Every week he would kill and pluck some of his birds for market, and many more near Christmas and other busy times. He had slaughtered thousands over the years. And when he plucked them he did it swiftly, expertly, and the soft flesh would not be bruised or torn when he finished. I've seen him kill and dress hundreds of birds. He was an artist.'

'How old was he', Wynford?' Mr Carrington asked.

'Not a lot older than I,' said my uncle. 'Seven or eight years. But that's a lot when you're young. He was already at work on the farm when I was a young boy visiting there.'

'What's he doing now?' asked Selby Davis.

'He's dead', my uncle said softly. 'Yes, he's dead these many years,' He shifted on his painted stool. He was far away, visiting an old sadness. 'He's been dead for years,' he repeated. 'One Christmas he had many geese, and he set to work early, day after day, killing and preparing them. The weather was intolerably cold. The mountains had a fall of snow, two feet deep and deeper in drift. It never stopped freezing. Night and day not a gust of wind – only the deep stillness of frost. My cousin kept the dead birds in a long barn, where they hung in rows, head down. The bitter cold worried my cousin. It was bringing in the wild things off the hills, the rats and foxes. He found himself slaying more and more near his filling barn.

'One night he awoke from sleep, bright awake at once, certain that something was wrong. It was just after three in the morning. He hurried into his thick clothes and wrapped a blanket over his shoulders. There wasn't a sound in the yard; even the living birds were silent. The brilliant snow threw back every gleam of light, redoubled it, so the night was unnaturally lit. The barn door was locked and safe. Nothing was out place. He opened the door and went in. The dead geese hung in their rows before him, untouched, pallid. The night was pitilessly still. My cousin moved along the stiff files, alert, waiting for something to happen.

'Then, in the cold barn, as if from high above him, he heard the call of geese, far away, the crying of wild geese out of the empty sky. He could hear them clearly, although he knew they were not there. He did not move. In an instant the barn was full of their loud honking; their flailing wings beat under the sturdy roof. He closed his eyes in terror, he wrapped his arms about his bent head, and through his barn flew the heavy skeins of great, invisible birds. Their crying filled his ears; the still air was buffeted by their plunging flight, on and on, until the last bodiless goose was flown and the long, wild voices were gone. He stood in the cold of his barn and opened his eyes. What he saw was this: he saw the hanging corpses of his own geese, every one swaying, every one swinging gently, And that was the most frightening of all.'

My uncle sighed. 'Poor old boy,' he said. Poor old lad. After a while they took him to Swansea, to the mental hospital, and he died there.

'How do you know this?' asked Ginty Willis.

'He told me,' said Uncle Wynford. 'I went down to see him, and he told me. He was a young man, only thirty-two when he died. He had killed thousands of geese, thousands of them.'

'What was his name, Uncle?' I asked. I stood in the warm day as cold as if I were in the heart of that long-dead winter and were standing under the roof among the swaying corpses of Christmas geese.

'Good God!' my uncle said. ' Are you still here? Get to school, get to school! You'll be late.' I turned and ran.

All day my friends were indolent in the heat of the quiet classroom, moving sleepily through their work, but all I could see were the high arrows of the streaming geese, all I could hear was their faint and melancholy crying, and the imagined winter was all about me.

PETER GRUFFYDD
Burial Of Strange Birds

In the presence of so much death we walked
among them with shock, those stiff bird
corpses littered row on ragged row.

A whole field gunned with dead, some packed
together near what had been a thorn-hedge lee
then was a raked swell of head-high snow.

Stalled in the blizzard's bared teeth
it seemed they had dropped as one dark sea,
a last gathering on wartime winter's heath.

Their red twig legs were raw as straws
on wind-bared ice, dry, drifted pathway
broken only by our steps creaky sound.

Too many years later I searched and found
what they might have been, migrants from Norway
that dips its nose in sea's glacial flaws.

They had rained from the night-sky,
ice coating feathers, flight wrecked by
that howling, demonic snow-wild.

Strange birds we had never seen, a portent
of some final freeze set to grip the world,
hold it to its last hours in gelid cold.

Nothing seemed as ominous or, in intent,
unforgiving as those shrivelled dead,
bettered down from flight over icy seas.

Would all the birds die, we wondered
callously, crushed by air which rimed
up feathers, iced the crushed trees?

Or was this an omen from the war, one
ultimate curt last word we should take
as given, could not survive again?

In the bare next field we'd begun to make
a snowman but stopped when someone placed
dun, rigid bodies in the pile's white dome.

We left them there, slit eyes withered,
on a kneeling mound only roughly shaped,
left to follow our clouding breath home.

R.S. THOMAS

Unity

What is Wales without its native tongue? I am a bird-watcher. Every autumn in Llŷn I love to watch the migratory birds flowing down the peninsula on their way south. Because of the wet summer and the persistent south-westerly winds, they did not come this year. It was a sad experience wandering over Mynydd Mawr in the early morning, and walking the lanes and hallows, without seeing any. It was like a museum. I told everyone: 'I remember how it used to be, the sky and lanes full'. It is a symbol of Llŷn without Welsh, the deadness would be there; beautiful names like Mynytho, Mellteyrn and Tudweiliog being mutilated by English lips.

Owls

...birds are hostile to the owl. And the owl is still called Blodeuwedd

The Mabinogion
Blodeuwedd

...Then he made for Caer Dathyl, and there were brought to him there all the good physicians that were found in Gwynedd. Long before the year's end he was whole. 'Lord, said he to Math son of Mathonwy, 'it is high time for me to have redress from him through whom I have suffered ill'. 'Faith,' said Math, 'he cannot continue thus, withholding thy redress.' ' Aye,' said he, 'the sooner I get redress the better I shall be pleased.'

Then they mustered Gwynedd and set out for Ardudwy. Gwydion travelled in the forefront and made for Mur Castell. Blodeuedd heard that they were coming, took her maidens with her and made for the mountain, and over Cynfael river they made for a court that was on the mountain. But through fear they could not proceed save with their faces looking backwards. And then, never a thing knew they before they fell into the lake, and were all drowned save she alone. And then Gwydion overtook her too, and he said to her: 'I will not slay thee. I will do to thee that which is worse; that is,' said he, 'I will let thee go in the form of a bird. And because of the dishonour thou hast done to Lleu Llaw Gyffes thou art never to dare show thy face in the light of day, and that through fear of all birds; and that there be enmity between thee and all birds, and that it be their nature to mob and molest thee wherever they may find thee; and that thou shalt not lose thy name, but that thou be for ever called Blodeuwedd.'

Blodeuwedd is 'owl' in the language of this present day. And for that reason birds are hostile to the owl. And the owl is still called Blodeuwedd.

Alan Garner
The Owl Service

'Gwydion. One of the Three Golden Shoemakers of the Isle of Britain. That's him.'

'What are you blathering at?' said Roger.

'He was the wizard who made the wife out of flowers for Lleu Llaw Gyffes. It's coming back to me. We had it read at school a couple of years ago. Gwydion made Blodeuwedd for Lleu, and she fell in love with Gronw Pebyr –'

'That's what Alison said.'

'And Gronw killed Lleu here on this very spot: then Lleu killed Gronw, and Blodeuwedd was turned into an owl –'

'The problem is to line the camera up with this hole, so that you can see the trees,' said Roger. 'But you have to be at least seven feet away, or you can't have the stone and the trees both in focus together. I want to use the rock texture as a frame for the trees in the distance. It should make an interesting composition.'

'Think of it, man!' said Gwyn. 'A woman made of flowers and then changed into an owl. The plates, man! It's all there if we could see it!'

Gillian Clarke
Blodeuwedd

Hours too soon a barn owl
broke from woodshadow.
Her white face rose
out of darkness
in a buttercup field.

Colourless and soundless, feathers
cream as meadowsweet
and oakflowers, condemned
to the night, to lie alone
with her sin.

Deprived too of afternoons
in the comfortable sisterhood
of women moving in kitchens
among cups, cloths and running
water while they talk,

as we three talk tonight
in Hendre, the journey over.
We pare and measure and stir,
heap washed apples in a bowl, recall
the day's work, our own fidelities.

Her night lament
beyond conversation,
the owl follows
her shadow like a cross
over the fields,

Blodeuwedd's ballad
where the long reach
of the peninsula
is black in a sea
aghast with gazing.

KATHY MILES

Woman Of Flowers (Blodeuwedd)

She is not made of meadowsweet,
conjured from broom and oak.

Her flowers are the jealous green stems
of roses, dark as poison-bottles,
bitter as taste of bark.

She drowns in nightshade
with its evening dreams of violence,
ivy's deadly sweetness.

Owl-change hunts her in
its monthly kill. She longs
to be flowers again, petal-scented,
falling to the strongness of a man.
Now she has birds' wisdom,
sweeps across dark landscapes,
she is predator, wants death;
claws sharpen in the evening holocaust.

Gladys Mary Coles

Augury

Blodeuwedd, The Mabinogion

Tall bedraggled pines, the day's incessant rain,
early nightfall and a river-road. You plunged
swift whiteness into the stream of light
intent on some small creature spotlit
on the camber, caught in my car's beams.
I felt your winged death impacting,
kept steady as you were woven in
becoming one with metal, rubber.
Not an everyday extinction. Born
of need, and one I saw as portent.
Next morning, cautious, tense,
I looked at last around the rim
of tyre, wheel-arch, finding you
translated
from feathers into fur into flowers.

And death followed three-fold.

Last night, one year later, your return
waiting on the wires, intent
close to the cottage eaves.
Your ululation as I arrived,
how you opened your wings like a cloak
to enfold me; how you became
one with the moon's translucency
your call dwindling into the blackness of Bryn Alyn.
Today, on the slate path to our door, I find
three gifts – your feather, white-tipped,
a dead but perfect fieldmouse,
a sprig of broom.

ELIN AP HYWEL
Owl Report

I'm glad to report that by now
things are starting to make some sense;
I'm beginning to get used to
birdishness.
(I've been feeling now, for a century or two,
that flying is getting easier, Co-ordination
between the right wing and the left has improved
and landing has become much, much smoother.
Aerodynamic. Yes, that's the word.)

It's a big step, looking back.
Sometimes, the past gets me by the gullet,
weighing down heavy.
a hard pellet, full of hair and bone.

especially on summer nights –
at that second, somewhere between twilight and dusk
when the world's a rush of wings in glory
and life's short as a mouse's memory-span,
a little, between one darkness and the next.

It's at times like these I remember:
I never did like the way
those multi-coloured silk gowns
used to stick to my sides in the heat
on those eternal afternoons
when Llew used to put his hand on my knee.

Feathers are really much better for you,
they're dry and light, like leaves or flowers:
they don't show the blood so much.
They're much, much easier to keep clean.

DUNCAN BUSH

The Snowy Owl

...The only thing he did want to show me was those birds in cases, and it was me who brought that up. I asked him about the one on top of the bookcase. Just you know, for something to say. He said it was a Golden Plover.

It's not a bird I think I've ever seen, I said.

No, he said. I don't suppose it is. Then he looked at me suddenly. Come upstairs a minute, he said. I'll show you something else. You can bring your drink. Hang on. Let's top you up.

But I covered the glass with my hand. I don't like to drink red wine at that time of the morning, especially when I'm driving. I'd have thought he would have offered me a glass of beer or something, as it was such a warm day. Or at least offered me a choice of something, instead of coming in with two poured glasses. I expect he had an opened bottle. Frankly, I'd have preferred water. I followed him up the stairs.

This is my study, he said. My point of production. He did pause for a moment then, as if to give us time to, you know, admire it.

You've got a few books, I said. They were piled in the corners under the slope of the roof, like they were holding up the bloody ceiling.

This is just some of them, he said. Most of it's just twenty years' worth of review copies. Postal freebies.

He took me across to this big glass-fronted case. There you are, he said. I'll bet you the price of that field you just sold me that you've never seen one of these before either. Not in the wild.

Well, I said. It's some kind of owl.

He nodded, looking at it. He said a name in Latin.

So what's that in English? I said.

It's a Snowy Owl, he said. He said it as if it was Jesus's shaving mug, with the razor and brush still in it. Or was, he said. Believe it or not, this one was shot in Breconshire, in nineteen hundred and two.

Is that a fact?

That's a fact.

I went close up. It must have stood over a foot tall on the perch. It was gripping this fir branch. On the floor there were some fir cones floured with snow. It had big yellow eyes. The feathers were pure white, with a sooty-brown mark in them like ermine, but more like a barring. It had furred claws.

God knows what brought it here, he said. They're almost unheard of in Britain. Perhaps there was an exceptionally hard winter, and it just came further and further south.

Looks like a fine specimen, I said. Probably worth a bit of money now, is it, something like this?

LESLIE NORRIS
Owls

The owls are flying. From hedge to hedge
Their deep-mouthed voices call the fields
Of England, stretching north and north,
To a sibilant hunt above ditches;
And small crawlers, bent in crevices, yield
Juice of their threaded veins, with

A small kernel of bones. It was earlier
I walked the lace of the sea at this south
Edge, walked froths of the fallen moon
Bare-legged in the autumn water
So cold it set my feet like stones
In its inches, and I feel on breath

And ankles the touch of the charged sea
Since. I saw in my lifting eyes the flat
Of this one country, north stretching,
And north. I saw its hills, the public light
Of its cities, and every blatant tree
Burning, with assembled autumn burning.

I know the same sun, in a turn
Of earth, will bring morning, grey
As gulls or mice to us. And I know

In my troubled night the owls fly
Over us, wings wide as England,
And their voices will never go away.

Gwyn Jones
Owl Of Cwm Cawlwyd

They came to the place where the Owl of Cwm Cawlwyd was. 'Owl of Cwm Cawlwyd,' Gwrhyr asked her, 'do you know anything of Mabon son of Modron, who was stolen away from his mother when he was three nights old?'

'If I did, I would tell you,' answered the Owl. 'When first I came to this place, this great valley you see was a wooded glen, but men came here and laid it waste. Then a second wood grew up and filled it, and in course of time yet a third; while as for me, why! the roots of my wings are become mere stumps. But from that first day to this I have heard nothing of the man you are asking after. However, I will be a guide to Arthur's messengers and bring you to the oldest creature God created in this world, and the one who has fared farthest afield.'

They came to the place where the Eagle of Gwernabwy was. 'Eagle of Gwernabwy,' Gwrhyr asked him, 'we are hopeful that you can tell us something of Mabon son of Modron, who was stolen away from his mother when he was three nights old.'

'When first I came to this place,' said the Eagle, 'I perched on a rock, and from the top of that rock I pecked at the stars each evening. It was so long ago that the rock is now not a hand-breadth in height, and yet from that first day to this I have never heard tell of him you are asking after.' As they were turning away, dismayed, the Eagle flapped his great wings wearily. 'Though once, I remember, I went hunting my food as far as the lake of Llyn Llyw, and when I reached there I sank my claws into a salmon, thinking he would be food for me for many a long day; but he was strong enough to drag me down into the depths of the lake, so that it was with difficulty I got away from him. Later he sent messengers, sewin and sea-trout, to make peace with me, and came to me in person to have fifty tridents plucked out of his back. Unless he knows something of what you ask, there is no one in the world who may. So if you wish, I will be your guide to the place where you may find him.'

They came to the place where the Salmon of Llyn Llyw was. 'Salmon of Llyn Llyw,' said the Eagle, 'here is your old friend and enemy, the Eagle of Gwernabwy, and these are Arthur's messengers.

T.H. Parry-Williams

Owl

Back home in Arfon, with nothing but the sound
Of the wind and the river and the lake's small ripple,
And sometimes the busybody bark of a hound,
Sudden and harsh, as someone crosses the hill;
Back home in Arfon, why should I make it my
Concern, whatever king may do or crank,
Or fear oppressors' frowns? Never has the cry
Of the base world come over the top of the bank...
As night closed in, boldly, without a care,
I strolled along the highway all alone,
Counting the pitch-black poles, each in a pair,
And the trilling wires, each one by one;
Between a prop and a pole, on a round pipe,
I saw an owl, – and felt terror's grip.

R. Williams Parry

The Owls

When night lit up the gleaming
Of dust along the road,
And at Pen Llyn the empty bridge
The placid stream bestrode,
I heard the owls from far below
Hooting through the groves in Cwm-y-Glo.

When the wild duck rode at anchor
And rocked beneath the moon,
And the forest mere in icy spray
Across their backs was strewn,
To the wind which roared on Mynydd Du
They made their answer piteously.

When the Glaslyn slid into a shadow,
Like a sword into its sheath,
And red the mansion windows burned
The rookeries beneath,
They cried when the dogs gave cry no more,
And night came down on Ynys-for.

And when the twilight wraps creation
After its demented day,
And over worker and the work
The voiceless hush holds sway,
Their tongue will have, I promise you,
Nor joy nor pain – Too-whit, too-whoo!

Elizabeth Saxon
Owls At Gregynog

There are owls tonight.
We cannot see them
but they call openly,
formidably identifiable.
demanding
a predictable response.

The cries of owls
define the sunlight
of the russet mornings
and all the delight
of trees and heathers
planted with such
conscious concern

for their informal
patterning.

These are mating calls
for more than the warm
fusion of a moment.
The wisdom of owls
is of contrast and shade,
is in part
the slow blink
of their own dreaming eyes
above their rending claws.

The owls are old.
Even the hills pause
for their call.
Poised and certain
owls pitch their cries
into the darkened rocks
which reverberate.

FRANCIS KILVERT
Ruth

Tuesday 8th Feb, 1870
From Wye Cliff to Pont Faen. Miss Child in great force. She showed me her clever drawings of horses and told me the adventures of the brown wood owl 'Ruth' which she took home from here last year. She wanted to call the owl 'Eve' but Mrs Bridge said it should be called 'Ruth'. She and her sister stranded in London at night went to London Bridge hotel (having missed the last train) with little money and no luggage except the owl in a basket. The owl hooted all night in spite of their putting it up the chimney, before the looking glass, under the bed-clothes, and in a circle of lighted candles which they hoped it would mistake for the sun. The owl went on hooting, upset the basket, got out and flew about the room. The chambermaid almost frightened to death dared not come inside the door. Miss Child asked the waiter to get some mice for 'Ruth' but none could be got.

R.S. THOMAS

Barn Owl

1
Mostly it is a pale
face hovering in the afterdraught
of the spirit, making both ends meet
on a scream. It is the breath
of the churchyard, the forming
of white frost in a believer,
when he would pray; it is soft
feathers camouflaging a machine.

It repeats itself year
after year in its offspring
the staring pupils it teaches
Its music to, that is the voice
of God in the darkness cursing himself
fiercely for his lack of love.

2
and there the owl happens
like white frost as
cruel and as silent
and the time on its
blank face is not
now so the dead
have nothing to go
by and are fast
or slow but never punctual
as the alarm is
over their bleached bones
of its night-strangled cry.

Leslie Norris

Barn Owl

Ernie Morgan found him, a small
Fur mitten inexplicably upright,
And hissing like a treble kettle
Beneath the tree he'd fallen from.
His bright eye frightened Ernie,
Who popped a rusty bucket over him
And ran for us. We kept him
In a backyard shed, perched
On the rung of a broken deck-chair,
Its canvas faded to his down's biscuit.
Men from the pits, their own childhood
Spent waste in the crippling earth,
Held him gently, brought him mice
From the wealth of our riddled tenements,
Saw that we understood his tenderness,
His tiny body under its puffed quilt,
Then left us alone. We called him Snowy.

He was never clumsy. He flew
From the first like a skilled moth,
Sifting the air with feathers,
Floating it softly to the place he wanted.
At dusk he'd stir, preen, stand
At the window-ledge, fly. It was
A catching of the heart to see him go.
Six months we kept him, saw him
Grow beautiful in a way each thought
His own knowledge. One afternoon, home
With pretended illness, I watched him
Leave. It was daylight. He lifted slowly
Over the Hughes's roof, his cream face calm,
And never came back. I saw this;
And tell it for the first time,
Having wanted to keep his mystery.

And would not say it now, but that
This morning, walking in Slindon woods
Before the sun, I found a barn owl
Dead in the rusty bracken.
He was not clumsy in his death,
His wings folded decently to him,
His plumes, unruffled orange,
Bore flawlessly their delicate patterning.
With a stick I turned him, not
Wishing to touch his feathery stiffness.
There was neither blood nor wound on him,
But for the savaged foot a scavenger
Had ripped. I saw the sinews.
I could have skewered them out
Like a common fowl's. Moving away
I was oppressed by him, thinking
Confusedly that down the generations
Of air this death was Snowy's
Emblematic messenger, that I should know
The meaning of it, the dead barn owl.

MEIC STEPHENS

Owl

Cariad, since you packed
your bags, said goodbye,
my sleep's been troubled
by a hooting owl; daylong
he roosts in the rafters
of this ramshackle house,
no bother to me much, but
makes his perch at night
upon my sill, keeping me
awake until it's dawn.

I have tried many ways
to rid me of this bird:
stood at the window, shone
a lamp, clapped my hands,
but he's not to be shood.
I lie upon our bed, watch
the beaked minutes pass,
shut the curtains, walk
from room to hooting room
until the welcome light.

Cariad, since you went
beyond my love's borders,
an owl troubles my sleep.

EDWARD THOMAS
The Owl

Downhill I came, hungry, and yet not starved;
Cold, yet had heat within me that was proof
Against the North wind; tired, yet so that rest
Had seemed the sweetest thing under a roof.

Then at the inn I had food, fire, and rest,
Knowing how hungry, cold, and tired was I.
All of the night was quite barred out except
An owl's cry, a most melancholy cry.

Shaken out long and clear upon the hill.
No merry note, nor cause of merriment,
But one telling me plain what I escaped
And others could not, that night, as in I went.

And salted was my food, and my repose,
Salted and sobered, too, by the bird's voice
Speaking for all who lay under the stars,
Soldiers and poor, unable to rejoice.

Daffydd ap Gwilyn

The Owl

A pity that the 'lovely' owl,
Cold and sickly, won't be silent.
She won't let me sing my prayer.
Won't be quiet whilst there are signs of stars.
I can't get (woe the forbidding)
Any sleep or chance of slumber.
A hunchback house of bats,
Its back against sharp rain[s] and snow[s].
Each night (I am bewitched a little)
In my ears (memory's pennies)
When I may close (the pain is most apparent)
My eyes (those lords of [great] respect)
This, the owl's song and owl's voice,
Her frequent screeching, guffawing,
And her sham poetry she recites –
This wakes me up: I have not slept!

From then (this is the way I am)
Until break of day, with such wretched zest,
She'll be singing, miserably howling
'Too-whit-too-whoo' – such lively gasping!
With great verve – by Anna's grandson –
She urges on the dogs of night.
She's a slut, with worthless two-hoots.
Large of head, perverse of call,
Broad of brow, with berry-crotch.
An old, wide-eyed mouse-catcher;
Busy, colourless and worthless,
With withered voice, and colour stained.
In ten woods her screeching's loud,
Woe for her song (a wooden-collared roebuck),
And her face (features of a gentle woman)
And her shape: she's the phantom of the birds.
Every bird attacks her – she's dirty and she's exiled:
Is it not strange that she's alive?

This one chatters on a hillside more
At night than does, in a wood, a nightingale.
By day she will not draw (a firm belief)
Her head from a sturdy hollow tree.
Eloquently she used to howl – I know her face:
She is a bird of Gwyn ap Nudd.
Garrulous owl that sings to thieves –
Bad luck to her tongue and tone!

That I may scare the owl away
From me, I have a song:
'Whilst I'm waiting for a frost
I'll set alight all ivies!'

Catherine Fisher
Blodeuwedd

When oak, I was unbending;
would never have stooped to this.
A thousand years' slow circles
rang from my hearts wood.
Through acorn and gall I saw you
stumble into the world.

When I was broom I was golden;
my spines the haunt of birds.
I hid nothing, had no guile;
wind and rain speared through me.
In tapestries I blossomed
between unicorn and lady.

When meadowsweet, I was innocent;
white froth of fields that are gone.
Spume of hedge uprooted,
of scent and butterflies.
Children and lovers watched Spitfires
through my creamy skies.

What have you made of me, wizards?
Out of me what have you formed?
Treacherous, a taloned hunter,
mutated into your fall.
The conditions that will cause death;
how is it I know them all?

Huw Jones
Old Austin

Put out to grass,
abandoned for a faster breed
that races along motorways.
In the field's workshop
ferns slowly spray him green
rain refills the tank.

Some nights
when a bright moon
switches on his headlights,
a badger squats behind the wheel
and taxies home a few owls
tipsy after a barn dance.

Birds of Prey

…and 'dilly dilly',
calls the soft hawk,
'Come and be killed.'

The Mabinogion
The Eagle Lleu

That night they went to sleep. And when the swineherd saw the light of day he roused Gwydion, and Gwydion rose and arrayed himself and came with him and stood beside the sty. The swineherd opened the sty. As soon as he opened it, lo, she leapt forth and set off at speed, and Gwydion followed her. And she went upstream and made for a valley which is now called Nantlleu, and there she slowed and fed. Gwydion came under the tree and looked to see what it was that the sow was feeding on. And he could see the sow feeding on rotten flesh and maggots. He then looked up into the top of the tree. And when he looked he could see an eagle in the tree top. And when the eagle shook himself the worms and the rotten flesh fell from him, and the sow eating them. And he thought that the eagle was Lleu, and sang an englyn:–

Grows an oak between two lakes.
Darkly shadowed sky and glen,
If I speak not falsely,
From Lleu's Flowers this doth come.

With that the eagle let himself down till he was in the middle of the tree. Then Gwydion sang another englyn:–

Grows an oak on upland plain,
Nor rain wets it, nor heat melts;
Nine score hardships hath he suffered
In its top, Lleu Llaw Gyffes.

And he let himself down till he was on the lowest branch of the tree. And he sang this englyn then:–

Grows an oak upon a steep,
The sanctuary of a fair lord;
If I speak not falsely,
LIeu will come into my lap.

And he alighted on Gwydion's knee. And then Gwydion struck him with the magic wand, so that he was in his own likeness. Yet none had ever seen a man a more pitiful sight than was on him. He was nothing but skin and bone.

Bryan Martin Davies
Lleu

You were an eagle,
from the time you were struck by the spear
on the banks of the River Cynfael,
until your hour of release,
line by line
englyn by englyn
from the oak tree
that grew between the two lakes.

For a long time
you were an eagle
and your death was dressed up in feathers.

After the treason in the shadow of the hill,
you flew away,
where?
Was it to some rockbound nesting-place,
sharpening your claws
like sharpening a spear
to wait for revenge
before flesh rotted
before worms fathered
and before you became no more,
then a stain of blood and feathers on the floor?

Or,
did you aim at the sun,
straining each nerve
working each ligament
before the flesh rotted
before the worms gathered
to reach the sudden mercy of your home
in the flame?

GWYN WILLIAMS
Eagle Of Pengwern

Eagle of Pengwern, grey-crested, tonight
its shriek is high,
eager for flesh I loved.

Eagle of Pengwern, grey-crested, tonight
its call is high,
eager for Cynddylan's flesh.

Eagle of Pengwern, grey-crested, tonight
its claw is high,
eager for flesh I love.

Eagle of Pengwern, it called far tonight,
it kept watch on men's blood;
Trenn shall be called a luckless town.

Eagle of Pengwern, it calls far tonight,
it feasts on men's blood;
Trenn shall be called a shining town.

GIRALDUS CAMBRENSIS
A Prophecy of War

According to vulgar tradition, these mountains are frequented by eagles who, perching on a fatal stone, every fifth holiday in order to satiate her hunger, with the carcasses of the slain, is said to expect war on that same day, and to have almost perforated the stone by cleaning and sharpening her beak.

GERARD MANLEY HOPKINS

The Windhover

To Christ our Lord

I caught this morning morning's minion, king-
dom of daylight's dauphin, dapple-dawn-drawn Falcon, in his riding
Of the rolling level underneath him steady air, and striding
High there, how he rung upon the rein of a wimpling wing
In his ecstasy! then off, off forth on swing,
As a skate's heel sweeps smooth on a bow-bend: the hurl and gliding
Rebuffed the big wind. My heart in hiding
Stirred for a bird, – the achieve of, the mastery of the thing!

Brute beauty and valour and act, oh, air, pride, plume here
Buckle! AND the fire that breaks from thee then, a billion
Times told lovelier, more dangerous, O my chevalier!

No wonder of it: sheer plod makes plough down sillion
Shine, and blue-bleak embers, ah my dear,
Fall, gall themselves, and gash gold-vermilion.

DYLAN THOMAS

Over Sir John's Hill

Over Sir John's hill,
The hawk on fire hangs still;
In a hoisted cloud, at drop of dusk, he pulls to his claws
And gallows, up the rays of his eyes the small birds of the bay
And the shrill child's play

Wars
Of the sparrows and such who swansing, dusk, in wrangling
hedges.
And blithely they squawk
To fiery tyburn over the wrestle of elms until
The flash the noosed hawk
Crashes, and slowly the fishing holy stalking heron
In the river Towy below bows his tilted headstone.

Flash, and the plumes crack,
And a black cap of jack-
Daws Sir John's just hill dons, and again the gulled birds
hare
To the hawk on fire, the halter height, over Towy's fins,
In a whack of wind.
There
Where the elegiac fisherbird stabs and paddles
In the pebbly dab-filled
Shallow and sedge, and 'dilly dilly,' calls the loft hawk,
'Come and be killed,'
I open the leaves of the water at a passage
Of psalms and shadows among the pincered sandcrabs
prancing

And read, in a shell,
Death clear as a buoy's bell:
All praise of the hawk on fire in hawk-eyed dusk be sung,
When his viperish fuse hangs looped with flames under the
brand
Wing, and blest shall
Young
Green chickens of the bay and bushes cluck, 'dilly dilly,
Come let us die.'
We grieve as the blithe birds, never again, leave shingle
and elm,
The heron and I,
I young Aesop fabling to the near night by the dingle
Of eels, saint heron hymning in the shell-hung distant

Crystal harbour vale
Where the sea cobbles sail,
And wharves of water where the walls dance and the white
cranes stilt.
It is the heron and I, under judging Sir John's elmed
Hill, tell-tale the knelled
Guilt
Of the led-astray birds whom God, for their breast of
whistles,
Have mercy on,
God in his whirlwind silence save, who marks the sparrows
hail,
For their souls' song.
Now the heron grieves in the weeded verge. Through
windows
Of dusk and water I see the tilting whispering

Heron, mirrored, go,
As the snapt feathers snow,
Fishing in the tear of the Towy. Only a hoot owl
Hollows, a grassblade blown in cupped hands, in the looted
elms
And no green cocks or hens
Shout
Now on Sir John's hill. The heron, ankling the scaly
Lowlands of the waves,
Makes all the music; and I who hear the tune of the slow,
Wear-willow river, grave,
Before the lunge of the night, the notes on this time-shaken
Stone for the sake of the souls of the slain birds sailing.

Leslie Norris

Buzzard

With infinitely confident little variations of his finger-ends
He soothes the erratic winds.
He hangs on air's gap, then turns
On royal wing into his untouchable circle.
All, all, lie under his sifting eye,
The squat man, the sheep, the mouse in the slate cleft.

He is not without pity for he does not know pity.
He is a machine for killing; searchlight eye,
Immaculate wing, then talon and hook.
He kills without cruelty for he does not know cruelty.

If he fails in a small death he is awkward. And angry.
Loosing upon the hills his terrible, petulant cry.
To fail often is to die.
His livelihood is such single-minded and obsessional artistry.

He is not secluded by emotion
Or impeccable clear thought even
Into considerations other than his pure life.

We observe our prey doubtfully,
Behind many hedges in tufted country.
Even when we see it clear
Have too many words to kill it.

Tony Curtis

Pembrokeshire Buzzards

The buzzards of my boyhood days are back again,
their wide-stretched, ragged wings
like distant, emblematic kites. Our speed brings
them close to, still as icons, precisely drawn.

A single blown buzzard's egg nested in Pwllcrochan
at the centre of gull, wren and blackbird
in my shotgun-toting cousin's collection,
confined in the shoe-box under his bed.

For twenty years since then, in my middle time,
they were rare. It seemed they had gone too
the way of the plagued rabbits. The oily spew
of the refineries, the tourists' fumes

and farmers' chemicals had seen them off. But
now the buzzards of my growing years are back.
Each road, every deep, high-hedged track
is reigned over by a pair – imperious, vigilant.

Where did they go? All these years.
Somewhere unseen, perched high in pylons, poles and trees
their clawed, bobbing weight was riding always.
Above our speeding car, memories lift off the wires.

John Barnie

The Confirmation

It was a fine September morning. John stood on the Rholben, and thought again how the hills were like a flock of grazing beasts, heads down, moving towards the town. There he could see the rectangle of the swimming pool, a turquoise eye that blinked every now and then with a white splash as someone dived off the high board.

He walked on, like a tick bird on the shambling brown back of the hill. He stopped to look along the Rholben's western slope where the bracken was deep fox-red with a special intensity in the autumn light. He looked up, narrowing his eyes, at the sky.

High above was a falcon. As he looked, it closed its wings and fell, hurtling down as if to embrace the earth. It was defined only as a darkness against the light blue sky. With the speed of a stone, it disappeared amongst the bracken of the slope.

John expected something to happen, a screech, or the bird rising again. But he waited and nothing happened. The sky remained an empty forget-me-not. The slopes glowed with the bracken. He stood still and erect, a tick bird on the bony ridge of the hill, until he became aware of the wind tugging itself across the strands of barbed wire where a field wall had collapsed.

–Wooo wooo. Whooo ooo wooo.

Like the sounds of the dead. Nothing moved on the hill.

GLYN JONES

Esyllt

As he climbs down our hill, my kestrel rises,
Steering in silence up from five empty fields,
A smooth sun brushed brown across his shoulders,
Floating in wide circles, his warm wings stiff.
Their shadows cut; in new soft orange hunting boots
My lover crashes through the snapping bracken.

The still, gorse-hissing hill burns, brags gold broom's
Outcropping quartz; each touched bush spills dew.
Strangely, last moment's parting was never sad,
But unreal, like my promised years; less felt
Than this intense and silver snail calligraphy
Scrawled here in the Sun across these stones.

Why have I often wanted to cry out
More against his going when he has left my flesh
Only for the night? When he has gone out
Hot from my mother's kitchen, and my combs
Were on the table under the lamp, and the wind
Was banging the doors of the shed in the yard.

Gwynne Williams

The Wind Hawk

See above!
He slides
as on a sea of glass
casting the fear
of his bite
through the tumult of the woods
until the whole locality flees
in haste to cave or den
from the open meadow.

But all in vain!
He dives out of necessity
on his traditional bread
then
slowly
he rises on his way.
his breast
dripping with blood.
to vent his venom
once more
from the sun's ocean.

Phil Carradice

Merlin

A few hours later we were several miles distant, Arthur and me, free at last from the warband which was, even now, beginning to argue about their new leader. Poor addled Arthur skipped along beside me, happy to be out in the cold November air. Already Ambrosius Aurelianus was just a memory.

Beyond the Severn the blue slopes of the Welsh hills reared huge and solemn in the morning sunshine.

"Your home, Arthur," I said, pointing. "Your home from now on."

He grinned at me and gleefully wiped the spittle from his chin.

"Yes," he said. "Home."

Suddenly his head swung around, staring intently inland. I followed his gaze. Grey bellied hunting birds – hawks and falcons – were wheeling and dipping over the edge of the moor.

"Birds," whispered Arthur. "Pretty birds."

I smiled.

"Merlins, Arthur. They're called merlins. They're hunting for food. For their families. Taking it home to their nests."

"Merlins."

He repeated the name over and over again, relishing and tasting its sound. Then he smiled and I could have sworn there was cunning in the expression.

"You are my Merlin. You're taking me home. You are my Merlin, aren't you?"

I raised my eyebrows at him and slowly nodded my head.

"If you like, Arthur. I shall be your Merlin."

He danced down the track ahead of me, singing "Merlin, Merlin" at the top of his voice.

"And you," I whispered to myself as I walked after him, "shall be my king."

Gwyneth Lewis

Red Kites At Tregaron

They know where to find me when they want to feed.
At dusk I prepare, layout the fat

and spread unspeakable offal in snow
like scarlet necklaces. They know

how to find me. They are my words
for beauty and other birds

fight them, vulgar, down threads of air
which bring them to me. They brawl for hair,

for skin, torn giblets and gizzard which I
provide for them, domestic. Inside

the house is so cold I can see my breath,
my face in the polished oak. My mouth

is sweet with silence. Talon and claw
are tender to me, the craw

much kinder than men. What is most foul
in me kites love. At night I feel

their clear minds stirring in rowan and oak
out in the desert. I stroke

the counterpane, my sleepless skies
filled with the stars of untameable eyes.

Clyde Holmes
Hen Harriers

I
Delivered himself regularly
to the valley,
carried news of nothing
but his presence.

Daily I followed his spread
of wings as he read
the ground just beneath him,
finely tuned to each tussock.
Screens of flickering
light and shade showed him
real images of flesh and blood.

II
On a remote tarn
only his reflection
is wind-surfing;
water, his ruffled image.
He keels over, his wing –
waves conjured from the surface.

He shins up air,
slides down again
to his heather-bound mate;
she's fallen for his stunts
and the vigour
of his aerial limping.
A shot here would
shatter the sky dance.
For a few months
the blanket bog has an albatross.

III
We watched him spellbound.
Had he wished for a small portion
of cloud-shadow to tip,
like arrows, his snow-white wings,

so that he too could be
atoned: with wind, casting himself
over mountains, never missing
the quiver of his soft targets?

Or had his pledge been broken
and he condemned to a limbo
close to land, always
mobbed by his own black primaries?

ROBIN GWYNDAF
Ifor Bach's Eagles

Although very little is known about Ifor Bach, he was considered a leader of considerable courage. He once boasted that his twelve hundred men could defeat any twelve thousand of the enemy.

According to tradition Ifor Bach's treasure is kept in a deep vault in the castle at the opening of a tunnel leading to Cardiff Castle. The treasure is guarded day and night by three huge, ferocious eagles. At certain times of the year their unearthly screams terrorised the countryside and the noise of the flapping wings was like thunder. In the seventeenth and eighteenth centuries groups of armed men attempted to destroy the eagles, but without success. They were savagely attacked – even those whose arms had been blessed by a priest. No one will ever succeed in destroying the eagles, for they will stay in the castle to guard Ifor Bach's treasure until he returns with his 'twelve hundred men of Glamorgan'.

Mike Jenkins

Red Kite Over Heol Nanteos

Walking with my brother over a chalk escarpment
our separate childhoods miles of years away,
though bracken reminds us of Penparcau:
huge prehistoric ferns
a cavern of fronds
to conceal you in hide-and-seek
till everyone had gone.

We leave our past with them,
brown and flakey as old papers,
to follow paths by sycamores and beeches
by wind-sculpted oaks and precocious saplings:
talking two nations in a reservation
motorways have been told not to reach.

Laughter flies over the unmapped border
between us, his ears finely tuned
to birdsong which, to me, all merges into one.
He points out a willow-warbler,
common enough, yet its descending scale
is made virtuoso by his enthusiasm.

He tells of a red kite over Heol Nanteos,
circled in his sights
before he drove on.
Birds migrate for food and season,
he jets because of ambition:
exotic trilling and rainbowed plumes.
The red kite is rare, it is threatened,
so close to once our home.

Roland Mathias

Hawk

There are marks of snow on the goitred neck
Where the cut begins. Grey clouds concentrate
In a mountain hurly-burly shoulder
To shoulder. Buffet and Jehu-crack
Predominate. Slowly the day grows colder.

Already the cart-tracks are stiff and red
Pointing like chapped fingers from the gate.
Above the perfunctory grass a level,
Eye-flight off: look, close, rigid
A hawk, irate as a stone, with the squireen's cavil.

The flower's eye narrows, pupil-cold
To the master-pinion, nemesis over the heath.
A handful of lambs new-born and hardly
Able to stand or knuckle herd appaled
underneath. The span grows in the wind more lordly.

A nearby elm gives a warning creak.
The wind is stronger. Cruel, nonchalant
The grown spanshadow ascends, breasting
In smaller and smaller spirals, beak
Proper and cloudgallant, the black land cresting.

Out of terror only a speck that drives
Quickly before the wind to the shoulder line.
The tracks of the kingdom watch and the hammer
Stops under the hill. Each lamb unshrives
His fellow and fine the day is with a laverock shimmer.

Vernon Watkins

Kestrel

Kestrel, king of small hawks, moreover
Keenest of sight, blind wings you shake,
Pinned on the sky, and, quivering, hover

High over prey. A gloom you make
Hang from one point in changing time
On grass. Below you seawaves break

Rebellious, casting rhyme on rhyme
Vainly against the craggy world
From whose black death the ravens climb.

Stand then in storm; see fragments whirled
And pitched by waters to a place
Where wave on wave in mockery hurled

Shake the great sea-rock to its base.
And still the inviolate wing and claw
Hold chaos in the grip of grace.

High on the rock's grass verge you saw
Your quarry. You above that rock
Hung by inscrutable, patient law,

Motionless. Then you plunged, a block
Between that headland and the sky
Hiding you. Stalling in their flock

The startled herring-gulls gave cry
Sprung from a sea of beaten flame.
Bird of my wrist, inspired you fly.

Who dares to think the storm untame
Can hurt or master you whom I,
Gathering the doom of all who die,
Uplift, in every age, the same?

John Davies

Ray's Birds

Lunchtime, the way he tells it,
with Ray weightless, orbiting;
the forgotten planet Stress,
his chickens screech SOS
so he's off. Fox?
No, they're spun shuttlecocks
because just yards away
stands a peregrine falcon – on a jay
quivering, spread to take the spike.
Ray drifts dreamlike.
When the falcon lifts and its full load
drags it down, he lunges, rolls
to save the jay, jaycrazy,
grabs a leg. And sits up. Dazed,
he's got the falcon. Flared eyes
flash beak. Ray makes – crabwise
past the pigeon loft, on wings –
for his shed, shuffles in, gets string,
gets stabbed, ties one leg to a brick towed
clattering. Leaps out. Shed explodes.

"So what now, Ray?" That's Rosalie,
unacquainted with falconry.
His arm with clenched fist
lifts. Air swoops, glory clamps his wrist.
"What'll it eat?" is Ray's sole doubt,
who spends days not finding out
then tries pigeon, desperate. It's his.
For the peregrine another bloody quiz.
Chasing its eyes around, it picks
at the soft corpse, flicking
to feather it. And pecks. And tears
raw treasure – soon, compere
of the feast, Ray's killed another three.
His top racing birds look queasy.

The falcon though hops on his leather glove
to stare, his lethal turtledove.

Rosalie sums up, unflinching,
the whole strange thing:
"You've got to let it go".
The sky's big through that shed window,
Ray has had doubts. It's young,
so demandingly high-strung
he has no time to live in.
And he's running out of pigeon.
So he pulls the door, stands
back. Loud hoovering woodland,
an astonishment of light,
yank the fat bird right
through the cramped frame
of all that's tame
in the world of walls
out to a radiant, rayless windfall.

But Ray has wings still. Weeks later,
watching his fastest bird home straight
towards Bishop's Wood,
he'd fly too if he could.
End of a race. His timer's ready, best
time, the loft a homemade nest.
Ray's eyes
are full of sky.
Then, higher, he sees it, black
cross, black skyjack.
That falcon tapping its wings on air
plummets, hits foursquare
his pigeon gone south
before Ray can close his mouth.
And a puff of brown
feathers filters down.
Ray's there like a praying mantis.
Don't tell him I told you this.

Sheenagh Pugh
The Haggard And The Falconer

To make a hawk, he sits up and starves
with her; stays with her through the pangs,
the hooded blindness, the sleeplessness aching
in the bones: three days and nights. The effect,
oddly, is to bond them, as torturers
the world over could tell you. Afterwards
they're a team: she'll fly for him
and her own pleasure, wear his colours,
take food from his hand, save
her meat for him.

There are some, though,
that will not, and until she flies,
he has no way of knowing. A haggard
is a hawk that takes no partner
and shares nothing. Her keen eyes watch
her own chance; the dizzy vertical stoop
from the air, that catches the throat,
is for her; the kill her profit
and her delight.

So he sits,
light-headed, chilled with hunger,
watching her; awake wondering
what she is; whether he has her.
Some say a haggard is the fault
of the falconer; a want
of devotion; he mustn't fail her.
While she is making, he'll scarcely see
his wife: he went in briefly
two nights ago, before he started
the hawk. His wife, as usual,
lay unmoved, watching him
under her eyelids.

When he has gone, she gives
herself ecstasies, fetching, in the dark,
great raucous breaths, heart hammering,
bright-eyed, exhausted. She could show
him how, but she will not: her love life
needs no helpmate, and if you can fly,
why share it?

ALUN CILIE
Kestrel

Ended, the hovering and manoeuvring on high,
And he is a cold-mouthed carcass at my feet;
The king who kindled fear in fowls from the sky,
No more the robber's lust consumes his blood.
Faded the flame of the lean, despoiling look
On the lofty throne where he peered down the cwm,
The shadow fled that quivered on the glade,
And limp the nails that squeezed prey in their clamp.
And for me, no further need to fetch the gun
And squat long stretches by the chicken coop
To spy him sneaking through the hazel groves,
But I will have a hearty laugh at his end
And set him to hang on high to bear the cost
Of keeping watch in my stead atop his post.

Ron Berry

Peregrine Watching

Watching peregrines becomes obsessional. We logged almost 300 hours between the three of us. Allan and Doug are brothers; apart from the peregrine connection they seem to have little in common. I first saw the tiercel on 18th April, '79. He went bulleting down, up and crosswise, chivvying a pair of ravens who were feeding hefty youngsters in a nest around the massive frontal boss of a buttress, less than ten yards from the eyrie as it turned out. But we had to find a vantage point. At the edge of a block of conifers adjacent to the reservoir, an old sheepfold two pounds with walls higher than a man, and the ruins of a dwelling place where, maybe, shepherds of two centuries ago praised God via Williams Pantycelyn hymns. They prompted wonder, those monoglot shepherds, times having shifted from rustic jogtrot to space satellites.

The larger pound gave us a view of the whole escarpment. The eyrie was 300 yards away. We were obeying the first principle of pergrine-watching. On 19th April we did a combined watch of six hours. At 9.20 a.m. *two* tiercels and a falcon flew high above the water. Cross tracking arid swinging tangents; they vanished like bees in a tumbling moraine of northern cloud. We couldn't determine which tiercel was mated to the falcon.

I was back in the sheepfold by noon the following day. The tiercel came tight-winged from the left, arrowing below the skyline to a flat rock near a bark-skinned rowan. He stood there for 35 minutes. Then he flew out fast above the conifers, only to return a few minutes later to his perch. He took off at 3.15 p.m., winging along the waterside and over the dam wall. He came back to a moley tump above the central buttress. Now he ruffled his feathers, he preened assiduously, breast, rump, thighs, hooking up his carpels to comb through the fish-belly grey barring. He looked all fluffed out and humped; he'd taken a bath in the out-flow brook from the reservoir. Winnowing some white feathers from his breast, he stroked them off his beak. His throat shone like a soap advert. The yellow of his feet gleamed as if glycerined. He stopped preening at 4.30 p.m., although occasionally he roused or probed under a wing – the task of perfection.

John Lloyd
Thoughts Of Boyhood

Well I remember in my boyish hours
   Gazing with rapture on the fantailed kite
As hovering full o'er Brenknock's ivied tower
   Slowly he wheeled his solitary flight.

Now low, as though within the mirror clear
   Of Usk's fair bosom he his form admired;
Now like the tenant of some loftier sphere,
   A speck amid the far-off clouds retired.

And often in our blithest, noisiest mood,
   When yet unseen his shrill cry told him near,
Up-gazing that mysterious form we viewed
   With a long look of wonderment and fear.

Now 'mid the landscape is he seen no more
   Fanning his broad wings in the noontide sun,
Scared from his circuit on that customed shore
   By prowling keeper armed with trap and gun.

In lone Cwmserri where the thunder clouds,
   For so its name implies, delight to rest,
In the dark bosom of the Vunglas woods,
   Alike the spoilers robbed him of his nest.

Nor his alone seek: the bustling jay
   And playful squirrel too they vermin call;
Each harmless, helpless thing alike they slay
   To make a show along their kennel wall.

Hence will each year more dull our woods become,
   The tapping woodpecker, the chattering pie,
Now rarely heard; the whooping owl is dumb,
   The raven calls not to his mate on high.

Sea Birds

More terrible than

chaos, and we stand at

the edge of nothing.

How shall we know its

purpose, this wild bird.

Dafydd ap Gwilym

The Seagull

A fine gull on the tideflow,
All one white with moon or snow,
Your beauty's immaculate,
Shard like the sun, brine's gauntlet.
Buoyant you're on the deep flood,
A proud swift bird of fishfood.
You'd ride at anchor with me,
Hand in hand there, sea lily.
Like a letter, a bright earnest,
A nun you're on the tide's crest.

Right fame and far my dear has –
Oh, fly round tower and fortress,
Look if you can't see, seagull,
One bright as Eigr on that wall,
Say all my words together:
Let her choose me. Go to her.
If she's alone – though profit
With so rare a girl needs wit –
Greet her then: her servant, say,
Must, without her, die straightway.

She guards my life so wholly –
Ah friends, none prettier than she
Taliesin or the flattering lip
Or Merlin loved in courtship:
Cypris courted 'neath copper,*
Loveliness too perfect-fair.

Seagull, if that cheek you see,
Christendom's purest beauty,
Bring to me back fair welcome
Or that girl must be my doom.

* Alchemical pun

Glyn Jones

Dafydd's Seagull And The West Wind

Dafydd's Seagull Addresses Him

Sir, after all that sweet, cod
The soft soap and the maldod –
Moon-matcher, comber-lily,
Snow-semblanced nun of the sea! –
You made me, master, say yes
And try to find her fortress.
But rather, since White-as-pith
Lived miles from Aberystwyth,
And you wanted an answer
In a flash, hot-hearted sir,
I passed on your passion's Cry
*To the wind, my sub-*llatai,
My diving lover, my date,
My moth-soft-breathing playmate,
My perfume-picker, my tall
Tree-shudderer of crystal.

His Seagull Addresses The Wind

Wind, why could you not bring back
Some message for this maniac,
Some sign from that paragon
Up there beyond Pumlumon,
Some signal, relenting word?
Why leave his pleas unanswered?

Wind, my wings in ton-up dives
Buzzed on your barbs like beehives;
I felt on my taut midriff
And pinion-bones your soft biff,
As your back bronchoed the rings

Of my boisterous white buckings.
Contentious, and me a bridge,
Your reckless torrent – courage! –
Wrecked me, your blood-loud roarings
Crashed both arches of my wings.

Up sun-sloshed slopes your breath blows
A pilgrimage of shadows,
And, crowding above those stains,
White clouds, homers to mountains,
Their slow groping hands sightless,
You shepherd through the green press
Of peaks – you guide soft-fingered
Summit-fumblers, your blind herd.

Corn-ears clash, your brushing wings
Rouse their concerted peckings,
And sweep that albino sea
Black, the battling tall barley.

You, roaring forest-ghost, purr,
Roosting on boughs; your whisper,
In the jungle's throat, becomes
A rugger-roar of welcomes.
You sigh trees-full of pendant
Catkin-fringes in a slant,
Scattering sycamore keys
And ripe fire-blooms of poppies.
My wild wind, my gruff bellow,
Spoiler and boiler of boughs,
Why have you left me to face
Alone this mouth of menace?
Come, wind, from sodden mountains,
Drum down on him drenching rains,
Or else embrace his love-glow
Decked in your sea-coat of snow.

Siôn Phylip

The Seagull

Fair gull on the water's bank,
Bright-plumed breast, well-provided,
Hawk does not seize or pursue,
Water drown, nor man own you.
Nun feasting on the ocean,
Green sea's corners' coarse-voiced girl,
Thrusting wide through the lake's neck;
And then shaking a herring,
Salt water's clear white sunlight,
You're the banner of the shore.
The blessed godchild are you,
Below the bank, of Neptune:
A sorrow for you, the change
Of your life, cold your christening,
Brave white bird in rough waters,
Once a girl in a man's arms.

Halcyon, fair slim-browed maiden,
You were called in your kind land,
And after your man, good cause,
To the waves then you ventured,
And to the wild strait's seagull
You were changed, weak-footed bird.
You live, quick fish-feeding girl,
Below the slope and billows,
And the same cry for your mate
You screech loudly till doomsday.

Was there ever on the sea
A more submissive swimmer?
Hear my cry, wise and white-cloaked,
The hurt of the bare sea's bard:
My breast is pained with passion,
Pining for love of a girl.

Sea Birds

I have begged from my boyhood
That she'd make one tryst with me,
And the tryst was for today:
Great was grief, it was wasted.
Swim, forget not my complaint,
To the dear maiden's region;
Fly to the shore, brave brightness,
And say where I was held fast
By the mouth, no gentle wave,
Of rough Bermo, cold foaming,
In all moods a sorry spot,
A cold black sea for sailing.

I rose, I travelled as day was
Breaking towards that dear bright face.
Dawn came on a thorny seastrand,
A cold day from the south-east.
A foul wind winnowed gravel,
Stripping stones, the whirlwind's nest.
The signs grew darker with dawn,
Twrch Trwydd drenching the beaches.
Inky was the wind's gullet
Where the western wind draws breath.

Harsh is the shore in conflict
If the western inlet's rough:
The sea spews, turning rocks green,
From the east spews fresh water.
Deep heaves from the ocean-bed,
In pain the pale moon's swooning.
The green pond is heaved abroad,
A snake's heave, sick from surfeit.
Sad heave where I saw tide ebb,
Rain's drivel that came pouring,
Cold black bed between two slopes,
Salt-filled briny sea-water.
Furnace dregs, draff of hell-spit,
Mouth sucking drops from the stars,

A winter night's greedy mouth,
Greed on the face of night-time,
Crock-shaped wet-edged enclosure,
A ban between bard and girl,
Foul hollow gap, raging pit,
Foggy land's filthy cranny,
Cromlech of every sickness,
Narrow pit of the world's plagues.
The pit was the sea-pool's haunt,
High it leaped, pool of prickles.
As high as the shelf it climbs,
Spew of the storm-path's anguish.
It never ebbs, will not turn:
I could not cross the current.

Three waters could flow eastwards,
Three oceans, these are the ones:
The Euxin, where rain wets us,
The Adriatic, black look,
The flood that runs to Rhuddallt,
Ancient Noah's flood turned salt.
The water-gate at Bermo,
Tide and shelf, may it turn land!

Glyn Jones

The Seagull

(after Dafydd ap Gwilym)

Gracing the tide-warmth, this seagull,
The snow-semblanced, moon-matcher,
The sun-shard and sea-gauntlet
Floating, the immaculate loveliness.
The feathered one, fish fed, the swift-proud,
Is buoyant, breasting the combers.
Sea-lily, fly to this anchor to me,
Perch your webs on my hand.

You nun among ripples, habited
Brilliant as paper-work, come.
Girl-glorified you shall be, pandered to,
Gaining that castle mass, her fortalice.
Scout them out, seagull, those glowing battlements,
Reconnoitre her, the Eigr-complexioned.
Repeat my pleas, my citations, go
Girlward, gull, where I ache to be chosen.
She solus, pluck up courage, accost her,
Stress your finesse to the fastidious one;
Use honeyed diplomacy, hinting
I cannot remain extant without her.
I worship her, every particle worships!
Look, friends, not old Merddin, hot-hearted,
Not Taliesin the bright-browed, beheld
The superior of this one in loveliness.
Cypress-shapely, but derisive beneath
Her tangled crop of copper, gull,
O, when you eye all Christendom's
Loveliest cheek – this girl will bring
Annihilation upon me, should your answer
Sound, gull, no relenting note.

John Morris Jones

The Seagulls

On the shore as I was walking
    All my thought was still of thee;–
Came a cloud of seagulls skimming
    Gray and swift across the sea;

Gray-black birds that on a sudden
    Wheeled a moment in their flight;–
Straight the sun across them glancing
    Turned their wings to snowy white.

Once, I mind me, not a sunbeam
On my dreary days would fall;
Sudden blazed thy love upon them, –
White and glorious are they all!

Euros Bowen

The Gull

A bird's wing breaks
the lake's smooth surface,
and memory spreads
circles in the water,

one shape calls up another,
one dies to live in the other,

light settles in the shadow
and the shadow fashions light,

time repeats
the stir of horizons
between day and night,
repeats
the ferment featured in waters
between night and day,

then the circles
are seen
no more,
the lake calm,
the water still,
and the gull is away in the sky.

R.M. Lockley

Hoofti

In following a Great Circle the migrating bird may be guided by the set apparent movements of the sun, or of the star patterns, which occur hour by hour, day and night, season by season, throughout the year. Those set patterns which occur during the precise hours of the day or night when the bird is migrating along its Great Circle voyage in spring or autumn have, it may be argued, become fixed in the genetic make-up of the bird during aeons of evolutionary pressures through which the powerful impulse to migrate was developed during the gradual changes in world temperatures (advance and retreat of the polar ice-caps – which once covered Skokholm). It is true that the apparent courses of the sun and the major stars are not really fixed at all in the heavens, but so slowly do they alter that for man's navigational calculations they are regarded as static during each epoch. Any slight alteration takes a century of time, during which the visual changes could easily be registered in the genetical charts in the brain of the many generations of birds living through that ample period.

Farewell, then, Hoofti, may your long first flight under the stars and over the ocean from Skokholm, 6,000 nautical miles to the estuary of the River Plate, be a happy one. I hope I have unravelled a little of what goes on in that tiny head of yours! Forgive me if I have put there thoughts you never possessed. My critics will undoubtedly once more accuse me of anthropomorphism, and declare you are a mere machine, an automaton evolved by blind chance in the universal struggle for existence, that you no more than filled a niche awaiting an organism which could burrow under the earth, swim under the sea and fly from one summer to another, and live perpetually on little fishes. But is that adaptation not wonder enough? Ah, I have learned to respect and admire, even to love you, brave little bird that would peck my hand, determined to survive all hazards, when I came too near and interrupted that long soliloquy of your midnight watch, when you thought your strange thoughts, while the sea-wind tossed the fragments of baby-down still clinging to your glossy new feathers. For you have taught me a little honest truth, and stirred my imagination to decipher a little of the natural law; and I find no evil in you and your ways, but only much beauty.

Note: The author is writing here of the Shearwater.

Thomas Pennant
On Ynys Seiriol

Ynys Seiriol is about a mile long and bounded by precipices except the side opposite Penmon, and even there the ascent is very steep. The land slopes greatly from the summit to the edge of the precipices. During part of summer the whole swarms with birds of passage. The slope on the side is animated with puffin auks which incessantly squall round you, alight and disappear into their burrows, or come out, stand erect and gaze at you in a most grotesque manner, then take flight and either perform their evolutions about you or seek the sea in search of food. They appear first about the 5th or 10th of April but quit the place, almost to a bird, twice or thrice before they settle. Their first employ is in the forming of burrows, which falls to the share of the males who are so intent on the business as to suffer themselves at that time to be taken by the hand. Some few save themselves the trouble of forming holes and will dispossess the rabbits who, during the puffin season, retire to the other side of the island.

They lay one white egg. Males as well as females perform the office of sitting, relieving each other when they go to feed. The young are hatched in the beginning of July. The parents have the strongest affection for them but this affection ceases at the time of re-migration, about the 11th of August. They then go off, to a single bird, and leave behind the unfledged young of the later hatches as prey to the peregrine falcon which watched the mouth of the holes for their appearance, compelled as they must soon be by hunger to come out.

The food of these birds is sprats, or sea-weeds, which makes them excessively rank, yet the young are pickled and preserved by spices, and by some people much admired.

Christine Evans
Gannets

Gannets fall
as if fired back
by sky they have stretched
with their slow, strong wing-beats.

They swim up
in a smooth loose spiral
plumping the clearness
rhythmically under
them, kneading until the blue is
taut and trembling –

a cold, elated second, focussing.
One heartbeat, then turn
arrow heads down, folded back wings
plummeting down, plummeting in.

The black of each wingtip
sharp as a fin.

The dark water sends up its own wings
of white spray as it is pierced.
The bay vibrates with their soundings.

Far out on the west, their whiteness
signals the early simple message
sun, before any warmth
spills over the hunched shoulder
we were glad to lie against all night.

How high? A hundred feet, or more...
Depends how deep the shoal is feeding.

Until we tire of looking
they beat themselves a shaft of slippery air

like working up from sleep;
let themselves be sucked back down

to green drawling minutes under, and
being bounced out through
widening rings of effervescent light.
Gulping air again, and energy.

Over and over they plunge
straight down into the dark
to spear a glimpsed magnetic glitter.
Watching makes us hold our breath.

GWYN THOMAS
Seagulls

Whitenesses circles in sunlight,
Wheels of brilliant profusions,
Leisurely chains holding the sunshine
Or
Snowflakes spinning
Above the dump.

Landing on scraps of city life,
Breaking from the whorl of the great, white rings,
One at a time, and then rising.
Pecking, gorging on garbage–
Ash heaps, papers, potato skins,
Salmon tins, beans, tomatoes,
Meat begun to go maggoty,
The splotchy grey death of gravy–
Gorging, and then rising.

Rising to the links of purity,
The multiple twining white twists
In the sunshine's brilliant belt:
Seagulls in sunlight.

Thomas Pennant
A Wreck of Sea-Fowl

I continued my journey along the shore, which is for the most part flat, except where some small headlands jut into it. On this coast the Reverend *Mr. Hugh Davies,* of *Beaumaris,* was witness to a very uncommon wreck of sea-fowl, which had happened in 1776. He saw the beach for miles together, covered with dead birds, especially those kinds which annually visit the rocks in summer; such as puffins, Razor-bills, Guilemots, and Kittiwakes; of the last there were many many thousands. Numbers also of Tarrocks. And of birds which retire to distant countries to breed, were Gannets, Wild-geese, Bernacles, Brent-geese, Scoters, and Tufted ducks. The frost, from *January* 6th to *February* the 2nd, had been in that winter uncommonly severe: a storm had probably overtaken both the migrants and the remigrants, and occasioned this havock; and the birds, which are perpetually resident with us, underwent the same fate, unable to resist the freezing gale.

Anne Stevenson
Gannets Diving

The sea is dark
by virtue of its white lips;
the gannets, white,
by virtue of their dark wings.

Gannet into sea.

Cross the white bolt
with the dark bride.

Act of your name, Lord,
though it does not appear so
to you in the speared fish.

William Condry
Shearwatering

'Shearwatering' is a popular Bardsey pursuit. It is for dark nights only because shearwaters, fearful of predatory hawks and gulls, have learnt never to come to land by daylight or even by moonlight. On a still, warm evening we take the steep path up through the gorse to the top of Mynydd Enlli (Bardsey Mountain). There we sit and wait. We watch the summer twilight deepen and the mainland, two miles away, slowly fade until it becomes a long shadow floating on the sea. Then it vanishes. All is now dark about us and there is silence except for the far-off murmur of the tide in Bardsey Sound.

Faint and high overhead a strangled crowing. It dies away but returns, louder. It is joined by others until the air is full of wild shrieks, sobbings and wailings. Not dozens but hundreds of shearwaters have arrived for their nightly visit from the sea. We listen to their wings rustling in the darkness and soon we hear bird after bird thumping onto the turf all round us, sometimes at our feet. We switch on a torch. Now we can see them, quite sizeable black and white birds scuttling into burrows or just crouching on the ground. We easily pick them up, for on such a windless night they are unable to take flight unless they have a rock, a mound or a slope from which to launch themselves. For a few seconds I hold one in my hands and in the torchlight I see its soft dark eyes looking into mine. It tries to scratch me with the sharpened claws of its webbed feet. Then its long thin beak comes round and nips my wrist, fetching blood. When I put it down it scambles across the turf and up a bank. From there it flutters forwards, finding its wings and is gone into the night.

Mike Jenkins

Diver-Bird

People sat up from skin-baking or shade-seeking,
children in flabby lilos stopped squall-splashing:
not a pointy snorkeller, but a diver-bird.
'Duck!' someone called, as he dipped
and disappeared underwater, emerging
liquid minutes later as no human could.
'Guillemot', I said assured, chuckling.

Grey-black, shiny as wet seaweed
his head intent for rush of a shoal,
no periscope or radar could equal
that vision: beak needling fish
leading a feathery thread up and down.
I tried to swim out, follow him,
make clicking noises to draw his attention:
he ignored my performance.

Returning home, in reference books,
I realised 'guillemot' was just as absurd.
He was elusive here as he'd been
in the bay; no silhouette fitting.
Yet I knew he'd keep re-surfacing
further and further away, stitching
more firmly because I couldn't find a name.

The Nightingale

The air was warm
as a mouth
as thrush nightingales
began to sing

LESLIE NORRIS
Nightingales

I

My namesake, old Bill Norris, standing beneath a tree
So bitterly gnarled he might have grown from it, stopped
Talking to listen, lifted eyes dayblue and delighted.
And laughed a silent pleasure. 'There's a good many.'
He said, 'Walks past as close as you and never hears her,
Though she sings as bright in the hot noon as any night.'
Two feet above his head the dun bird pulsed and lilted.
It was in this village and perhaps for this same bird
I lay awake the whole of one miraculous darkness.
She sang so close to my house I could have touched
Her singing; I could not breathe through the aching silences.
And for nights after, hunched among pillows. I grabbed
At any sleep at all, hearing the nightingale
Hammer my plaintive rest with remorseless melody.
Full of resented ecstasy, I groaned nightlong in my bed.

II

Or driving one Sunday morning in Maytime Hampshire
On our way to a christening in one of the villages,
We stopped on Steep Hill, the road climbing headily upwards.
In the first warm air of the year we looked down on the
Trees, unmoving and full in the freshness of their leaves.
There were eight nightingales, eight, they filled the valley
With sobbing, the cataract of their voices fell
Erratically among the splendid beeches. Open-eyed
We stood on the lip of the hill, while near and far
The water-notes of their singing grew faint, were lost almost,
Answered and redoubled near at hand, trailed
Dropping sadly down the valley-sides, struck purely out
With sound round notes into the listening morning.
We were still with music, as the day was. That we were late
For the christening was to the credit of those nightingales.

III

When I was very young my father took me from bed,
Dressed me in haste, and we walked into the night,
Winter was so long gone I had forgotten darkness:
We went by paths which in daylight knew me well,
But now were strange with shadow. It was not long
Before we came to the wood where the nightingale sang,
The unbelievable bird who lived in the stories
Of almost my every book. Would it sing, would it sing?
I thought the wood was full of silent listeners.
I do not remember it singing. My father carried me home,
My head rolling back on its stalk at every measure
Of his deep stride, and all have brought back
From that long night are the fixed stars reeling.
It is the poet's bird, they say. Perhaps I took it home,
For here I am, raising my voice, scraping my throat raw again.

HARRI WEBB
The Nightingales

Once there were none and the dark air was dumb
Over the tree-stumps, the bare deforested hills.
They were a legend that the old bards had sung,
Gone now, like so much, so much.
But once I heard them drilling away the dark,
Llandaf was loud with them all of a summer's night
And the great Garth rose like a rock from their storm.
This most of all I desire: to hear the nightingales
Not by Taff only but by all our streams,
Black Rhymni, sullen Ogwr, dirty Ebbw
Dishonoured Tawe and all our sewered drabs.
And others whose names are an unvisited music
(Wales, Wales, who can know all your rivers?)
The nightingales singing beyond the Teifi,
By Aeron, Ystwyth, Rheidol, and those secret waters
The Beacons hold: Rhiangoll, Tarrell, Crawnon,
By Hepste and Mellte outstanding Scwd Einion Gam

(But let them not sing by Elan, Claerwen, Fyrnwy
Or Tryweryn of the Shame.)
You who have out sung all our dead poets,
Or them again in Cwm Prysor and Dyffryn Ceiriog,
And humble Gwydderig and Creidiol, do not forget them.
And that good man, no poet, who gave us a song
Even sweeter than yours, sing for him at Llanrhaeadr,
And in Glyndyfrdwy, what need to tell you to sing?
Sing in the faded lands, Maelienydd and Elfael,
And in the plundered cantrefs that have no name.
Come back and sing to us, we have waited too long,
For too long have not been worth singing for.
The magic birds that sang for heroes in Harlech
And hushed to wonder the wild Ardudwy sea
And they of Safaddan that sing only for princes,
We cannot call them again, but come you
And fill our hearts like the hearts of other men.
Shall we hear you again soon, soon?

ALUN

Song To The Nightingale

When our dear earth is hid by night
    Under its black wing,
The woodland choir is mute, but you
    Then gently sing,
And if against your heart a thorn
    Throbs beneath your breast,
You, till generous day should break,
    Will but sing, and leave the rest.

And like you is this gentle girl,
    Partner more than rubies dear,
At sunset, though across the land
    A thousand clouds appear,
When all day's comforters are dumb
    Her fidelity's complete;

In the night's anguish and dismay
Never sounded voice so sweet.

Though the worry almost numbs her heart
She'll not complain
Nor tire her dear ones with distress –
Her smile hides her pain;
Nor ends her song the long night through
Until bright hope shall dawn,
Shining like an eye of gold
Through the clear lids of morn.

EUROS BOWEN

The Nightingale

Was the nightingale killed in the groves?...
We heard the heart rise with her syllables
Up the stairs of quiet splendours,–
Passion voicing the flesh's scents
And enticing the ear to caress the poem:
The bird's vitality colouring night's bed
With roses, violets and the lily,
And the song in the warm, tight concealment of leaves
Makes the rod to blossom under the lips of stars.
We heard the uninhabited places in the sap of branches
Crushing the brain, drying up the breath,
And the trunk in the ground's stranglehold
Is rough with the thorns' bites,
So that fruit did not rain on the treetop
And so that taste did not fall on the bud,
Totally, expressively full,
Shining and consonantal from the round throat...
Is flesh hardening like an empty nut?
Is the wine in the glasses nothing but a stain?
Is the world from now on emptied of its intoxication?

H. THORNHILL TIMMINS
St David and the Nightingale

Even the nightingale, though a *rara avis* in these parts, has, this phenomenal season, been heard in the woods near Cresselly. The following tradition explains how these little songsters came to shun the county of Pembroke. It appears that St David, 'being seriously occupied in the night tyme in his diverse orizons, was soe troubled with the swete tuninges of the Nightingall as that he praied unto th'Almightie that, from that tyme forward, there might never a Nightingall sing within his Dioces; and this was the cause of confininge of the bird out of this countrey. Thus much,' remarks the chronicler, 'to recreat the reader's spirettes.'

WILLIAM CONDRY
An Absent Voice

From the woodlands of all Wales there is one regrettably absent voice – the nightingale's, a fact that has always fascinated people.Giraldus in the twelfth century observed how closely the edge of the nightingale's range coincided with the boundary between England and Wales and he quotes his travelling companion Archbishop Baldwin who wasn't altogether enjoying their tour of Wales. 'The nightingale', said the archbishop acidly, 'followed wise counsel and never came into Wales'. And Alexander Neckam, probably a little earlier than Giraldus, had written of a Welsh river (it could only have been the lower Wye) which had nightingales on one bank but not on the other.

The frontier of the nightingale's range is known to have fluctuated over the past hundred years or so. Numbers were evidently high in 1845 when a writer in *The Zoologist* reported: 'It is found plentifully in Monmouthshire, as I know, having heard the woods on the banks of the Wye about Tintern Abbey resound with its beautiful melody last May. It certainly is a singular fact if it does not step over into Glamorgan or Breconshire'. This it assuredly did from time to time. In 1900 Geoffrey Ingram, camping on the southern slopes of Caerphilly

Mountain, north of Cardiff, had several nightingales feeding daily on breadcrumbs outside his tent. In the same year nightingales were breeding at Cowbridge, thirty miles west of the Wye, having increased during the previous ten years. Further north too, the nightingale had advanced up the Severn into Wales and reached the Newtown area by about 1903.

For several decades the nightingale prospered. In 1928 Morrey Salmoh could hear five singing within half a mile of where he lived at Cyncoed, then partly wooded but now a built-up suburb of Cardiff. But the nightingale never became common enough to be taken for granted anywhere in Wales. In fact some years ago when the press reported one singing nightly in a wood in north-east Wales, so many people went to hear it that there was even a hot-dog stall in attendance. Such is the nightingale's charisma, conferred upon it by the ancient poets, then taken up again by those of the Middle Ages both on the Continent and in England. Not to be outdone the Welsh bards also celebrated this famous night songster though it is unlikely any of them ever heard it singing in Wales. *Eos*, an ancient name, was the word they chose for the nightingale, and *eos* also crept into place names that are still in use in districts where there are certainly no nightingales now and probably never were.

JOHN BARNIE
That Summer

The air was warm as a mouth
as thrush nightingales began to sing
near the house; which bush? which bush?
no one could say, standing there listening

while summer lightning brushed the earth
with blonde hair kilometers off
and unheard; the nightingales whistling
for themselves were experimental not melodic;

why should they be? these
were not the flutes of Chinese poets
drunk in the hills, playing how flawed
life is; after that summer they never returned;

we listened but the bushes were bushes
not the sounding board of invisible
instruments, and the lightning was an electric discharge
power-jumping to and from the fields.

MARGIAD EVANS

Evocative Voice

And, as she sat there she suddenly became aware of the nightingale's singing that was streaming out from an oak tree, and the tree was covered and all lit up with greeny-gold flowers like moss, which she was curious to touch. But she would not frighten the song, she said. They were right; the bird had flown from the party; it had flown to her because here in her native place she was invisible and quiet.

It was so whole, so perfectly beautiful, the song, that at first she was lost in it, her mind silenced. The first break of notes came fast and wildly, at unbelievably intricate speed, running downhill; then that was followed by three or four clear staccato calls, when the song brought itself up by its own command. Then the bird really began. Long, smooth cadences were laid upon the air, were stroked out to their shining tips, were divided thought by thought until it became impossible for the listener to decide which was the harmony – the sounds themselves or the inset pauses let into the voice. Yet it was not 'music'. There could be no human term for it, no comprehending what made the arrangement of the tones. Then for a short while, as by decision, it ceased, and Miss Boyce breathed.

She knew it would begin again. She knew it would not be over, for the world was charged with it. And, on the brink of its return, there whirled in the silence of her ears, a tintillation as of light, as of shining discs still turning and hovering on the thread of that vibration. Her first thought was to call the others, but she glanced at them, and did not. Why should she, she said; who cared? And at that moment the bird picked up its song once more, and again differently.

This time, it spent its phrases slowly, with melancholy distinctness, with a sort of sad eagerness, like a gambler who sees his gold dwindling. The notes were intricate at times, and were met by a piercing echo, out of the ground or sky, which joined to them without seam, and lengthened them to a sensitiveness unbelievable. The 'music' was now far more evocative: she did not know it, but already her few moments of pure listening were over, and her mind was acting scenes again. Now the beautiful sounds had become only another illustration of her passion's series of possibilities, as everything else that was lovely in the land and trees and skies.

Garden Birds

A slow singer, but
loading every phrase
With history's
overtones, love, joy
And grief learned
by his dark tribe…

Dafydd ap Gwilym

The Thrush

Music of a thrush, clearbright
Lovable language of light,
Heard I under a birchtree
Yesterday, all grace and glee –
Was ever so sweet a thing
Fine-plaited as his whistling?

Matins, he reads the lesson,
A chasuble of plumage on.
His cry from a grove, his brightshout
Over countrysides rings out,
Hill prophet, maker of moods,
Passion's bright bard of glenwoods.
Every voice of the brookside
Sings he, in his darling pride,
Every sweet-metred love-ode,
Every song and organ mode,
Competing for a truelove,
Every catch for woman's love.
Preacher and reader of lore,
Sweet and clear, inspired rapture,
Bard of Ovid's faultless rhyme,
Chief prelate mild of Springtime.

From his birch, where lovers throng,
Author of the wood's birdsong,
Merrily the glade re-echoes –
Rhymes and metres of love he knows.
He on hazel sings so well
Through cloistered trees (winged angel)
Hardly a bird of Eden
Had by rote remembered then
How to recite what headlong
Passion made him do with song.

Llywelyn Goch ap Meurig Hen

The Tit

Go now, bird, urbane and civil,
Tomtit with the piping bill,
From the South to my sweetheart –
That dear she that shared my heart.

To Merioneth run straightway,
Bright sound in the thorns of May,
Swift above bridges of copse,
Rider on the strong birchtops.
Plaintive grey beak, and tired wing,
Four colours to your tinting –
Green and blue, a lad who'd lief,
Black and white, tend on green leaf.
You, companion of the young,
Though tiny, bard of woodsong,
Are spry, little grey-cheeked bird,
Adept at secret concord,
Rush like the wind, luck's courtier,
To Merioneth to my dear.
Work your wings, master of idiom,
Toil above the forests' gloom:
Light on that fair form, and say
Unto Dafydd's wife, Good-day!

For my sake (she was my dear)
Ask her in her gold chamber
(Merioneth's bright as billow)
Not by day or night to go,
My second soul, gold-plaited

Modest girl, to Eiddig's bed.
Also, proud squire and sportive,
Wildwood poet hawks let live,
Possessing in your heart's-ease

Two slim feet, farers in trees,
Now be bold, match my desire,
Be bold to my soul's sister!

Say, author, diligent bird,
In pain's hour, woodland wizard,
My brother, that I've sung forth
To greet her from Deheubarth
And sevenfold anguish suffer
And barbs of longing for her.

Because, near the shining towers,
I've not seen her bright features –
Plead, bird, my winning praises –
Strange I've lived, this thirty days!

ANNE CLUYSENAAR
The Wagtail

Two days ago, and I still see him
landing in the stream in the evening sun;
flip, flip, snatching a midge
(it must be) out of the warm air.
Often, before, I've seen him. This time,
a silence in the high sweet sound of the stream
seemed to form where he was. I could see
there must be sounds: feathers, midge-whirr,
beak-snap, claws on the slippery stones.
Things he was hearing, and I wasn't.

Because of the intensity of that silence,
he still flips here, in my head, in the stream,
and I can visit the place with something like sight.

Mike Jenkins
Odd Bird

My son's bedroom, a square safety-pane:
a chaffinch was crashing again and again
in frenzied attack, wanting in.
Disturbing, it beaked at glass
our second skin, leaving it marked
with white wounds. This spangled
bird of our temperate climate
we talked of as some portent
some mad beast who'd get in
and whirl around a shrunken orbit
shitting on bright bedspreads:
who'd possess inside, send me scurrying
for odd means of capture, a basket
or a broom. My wife saw his dirt
on the sill as a personal insult.
I suggested the hanging mobile
might seem like a friend.
My daughter perfectly mimed
his curious eyes, searching head.
My son, less tame but more logical,
said it was his reflection.

We pulled curtains on the day
and sure enough, by evening's return
there was the chaffinch dancing again,
prancing against garage-window this time,
following in his solitary way
up and down, that other bird he saw
and couldn't reach, trapped forever.
His white flashes petalled
in leafy reds of his plumes;
he turned away, perturbed
and even dropped a morsel to begin
again that exhausting display
beating himself against an image of his own.

Margiad Evans

A Sparrow Singing

A sparrow singing! what surprise!
He knows the day has come,
He feels the force which lifts the skies
Though I feel none;
Though he of all the birds which rise
Alone tells light to senses numb
With weight of snow. It mystifies
To hear earth choose so slight a song
So carelessly, when all sound lies
Yet unbreathed on.

R.S. Thomas

A Blackbird Singing

It seems wrong that out of this bird,
Black, bold, a suggestion of dark
Places about it, there yet should come
Such rich music, as though the notes'
Ore were changed to a rare metal
At one touch of that bright bill.

You have heard it often, alone at your desk
In a green April, your mind drawn
Away from its work by sweet disturbance
Of the mild evening outside your room.

A slow singer, but loading each phrase
With history's overtones, love, joy
And grief learned by his dark tribe
In other orchards and passed on
Instinctively as they are now,
But fresh always with new tears.

Ruth Bidgood

Blue Tit Feeding

Early at the window in starved winter
a little knot of energies, a beaky hunger
fluffed and sleeked, taps, prises
unsucculent scraps of cracked putty,
swallows with a ripple of tiny throat.

Behind it climbs a bleak pale hill
stained with rust of December bracken.
White morning moon is barely seen
on hardly darker sky that seems
opaque, a barrier against pressure
of immensities. Imperceptibly
the chill day flows out to black deeps.

The blue tit pauses in its arid feeding,
flirts a crisp wing. Half-handful of warmth,
it stays for a moment still,
compellingly centre-stage, diminishing
to a backdrop the hill, dull morning sky,
pale echo of moon, black vertiginous
trenches of space-ocean, myriads
of molten and frozen, dying and rising worlds.

MARGIAD EVANS
A Wild Boy

It was a sunless afternoon, close and scented. The white butterfly, early hatched, was half blown, half lifted over the thick golden gorse. Two blackbirds were singing from opposite sides of the valley. 'Tee oh tee!' they sang, and waited, singing carelessly and listening intently as if only when it left their happy breasts had the song a value for them. Of all the birds I think they are the ones whose voices come nearest to our idea of music. In between the flourishes which pierce miles of distance, undulating with the hills, there are none of those strident intervals with which the thrushes contrast their purer notes. Perhaps the thrush is the greater musician. The blackbird is a wild boy while he sings, but having sung he seems to listen to his notes travelling over the earth with an intense and detached wonder expressed in his silent poise.

It made me smile, it made me laugh to hear those birds!

The thrush: 'All *right* then.' And passionately: 'I don't *believe* it.'

'Chee-chee-chee-chee-women's institute!' rattled a chaffinch. This is Sian's interpretation of his comical gush, and since she pointed it out, I have always thought it the most distinct articulation in bird sound.

'Tee oh tee!' Repeated the blackbird buoyantly. Then all the little birds began whirring and chipping, and the cuckoo pendulum swung against the horizon wall. Finches and wrens and robins, pippets, linnets, yellow-hammers were all grinding and sharpening their small notes, like a workshop, where harsh magpies swore and woodpeckers laughed madly against their own tapping.

'Cheat-cheat-cheat!' cried a little unseen voice. And I heard a little sturdy note clanging from the ivy-curtained undergrowth over and over again – the blacksmith bird. But above all the blackbird, the idle beauty, lost in singing and the for ever too late effort to regain what he had sung!

John Ormond
Homing Pigeons

Out of a parsimony of space unclenched,
Into the not known and yet familiar,
They ascend out of their hunger, venture
A few tentative arcs, donate new
Circumflexions to the order of strange sky;
Then blend to a common tangent and so render
Themselves to the essence of what they are.
What beguilement shepherds the heart home?
Not what we know but some late lode-stone
Which, far, was always there, drawing us
To a meaning irreducible, to a fixed star.

Why then the falling, all the fumbling
As tumbler pigeons, fools flying, with the most
Inept of masteries? But flying still
And, despite awkwardness, being, as best we can,
Committed, in the chance weather we approach,
To what and where, without a sense of reward,
We may reach and trust to be fed.

Game and Farm Birds

kid kid kid kootje
kid kid kid kootje

Jean Earle
Dancing Pheasants

Under the white peak,
A watcher.

A naked field where two birds,
Ruby-and-topaz mantles pricked,
Scrape their big feet.

The watcher, frozen; but in bird blood,
Primeval fires.

They dance; and the watcher smiles,
Deep in his snowy heart...
So the near-men
May have learned smiling
When they began to dance
Through watching the birds

That were evolving from dinosaurs.
Shag woods –
So long sunken
Not a fossil returns –
In overlaps of time
Might have concealed both the first men
And the last dragons?

The little dragons
(That were almost birds)
Danced in their spring scales,
Mutive to feathers –
While the monkeyish men
Peered from defensive covers
As men do still
And they smiled.

What has changed? Not the scrape dance-floor,
The watcher – who has always twitched
His atavistic smile. Huff, puff and burnish –
A formal lust,
Ritualised – pursued
Even to death's bloody bow

While the dun hen, spring after spring,
Loses eggs to the crow.

Myriad transitions, varying only
The outward forms.
No mid-quick changes...

Not cock nature
Nor the hen's steady plan
For the one egg left.

Least of all –
Oh, least of all, first-and-last men.

George Borrow

Feeding the Saxons

We left the brook on our left hand and passed by some ruined walls which my guide informed me had once belonged to houses but were now used as sheep-folds.After walking several miles, according to my computation, we began to ascend a considerable elevation covered with brown heath and ling. As we went on the dogs frequently put up a bird of a black colour, which flew away with a sharp whirring.

"What bird is that?" said I.

"*Ceiliog y grug*, the cock of the heath" replied my guide." It is said to be very good eating, but I have never tasted it. The *ceiliog y grug* is not food for the like of me. It goes to feed the rich Saxons."

Ceiliog y grug *is a reference to the red grouse.*

ALUN LLWYD
Geese

On New Year's Eve, one could hear their red scream
in the stable, and the wings beating still
in the grasp of death,
and the blood, dripping from a round hole,
flowed like foam under the door.

Innocent of their fate,
they could be seen swaggering on the farmyard
and on the fields, or waddling
in a stupid, babbling host;
loose-tongued, drunken geese
cackling like quarrelsome old women,
their supple speech without restraint,
and their postures arrogant;
geese grazing in the fields for a lifetime
or paddling in pools.

One by one they would be pursued
from the field, set on by dogs;
the flexible nape would be bent
in the damp stable,
bent before the feathers were plucked,
and the young goose
hissed and screamed like bagpipes in my father's
armpit, before the cold blade
of his scissors scraped clumsily through the bone,
and opened a hole in the head.

The thin-naped geese dangled by their feet
as limp as clothes on the clothes-line;
it took us to nightfall
plucking the feathers and scorching the skin,
and the snatched snow grew on the ground;
the stable's floor was stained by wounds,

and the feathers, mingling with the blood,
were as white foam fuming red in the sunset,
and scoured, they were placed on the scales.

On the break of day the next day
the hoarfrost of January
bled like feathers.

R. WILLIAMS PARRY
The Geese

Through the crests of trees December
Made the saddest uproar ever,
Like waves breaking.

A field's corner lay below,
And there, with not a thought of woe,
The geese were grazing.

Like feathers the leaves multiplied,
Black, blood-coloured, pied,
On the green of the dale.

And in the sight and sound of death
I spelt out to the birds beneath
The branches' tale.

"And therefore do not still delay
But on your broad wings flyaway
Before the moment
Comes when the good woman goes
With goods of butter, cheese, and geese
To the Great Market."

But fie on all such lies as these!
A contemptuous parade of geese
Was formed in order.

And then there came the constant crackle
Of their single-minded foolish cackle
Over and over.

EMYR HUMPHREYS

Turkeys In Wales

Tenders are invited for the supply of turkeys to County Council Establishments.

Gwent County Council, September 13, 1975

Certain turkeys survive
They believe in their exemption
Attribute
Their extra days
To the music
Of their eloquence
And their influence
With the Owners.

Their cold combs
Are colourless and flaccid
Their long necks
Shredded with age
Their feet are decorated
Like their feathers
With fading orders
And birthday honours.

They consider the stony field
A sphere of influence
Or at the least
A corner of comfortable exile
Reserved for their survival
The hungry young

Observe them
And the brightness of the seed corn
Those tireless beaks
Gobble with horny care.

Such birds
They whisper between themselves
Consume the last lumps
Of our sunlight

While comrades in fresh feathers
Are snatched
And sacrificed

If we had hands
We could learn
To turn
Necks into wreaths.

Peter Finch

Scaring Hens

kid kid kid kootje
kid kid kid kootje
kootje
    kutch
kootjie
    kutch kutch
kootjie
good-chick
good good
good-chick
good good good
good-chick
ha cudies, kud-dids, cudies, cuddles,
cud-ducks, kud-chuck, diddles, doddles,

cuddles, gidi-gidi cuddles,
good good, gidi-gidi,
gidi gidi, gud gud,
gwd gwd
good good
    good good
good
CUT CHICK CUT CHICKS
KWIT KWIT
CUT GOOTCH
GOOTCH CUTCH CUT CUT
gootch gootch cut coo
cwtch (goots)
gwsh
    jee cootch coo
coo coo cootch
    cwtsh cwtsh cwtsh
cwtsh cwtsh cwtsh
wheeeeeeeeeeeeeeeee
wishsh got got
whist got cot cot
cot got cot cot
cot cot got cot
KWIT CUT CHICK
KWIT
goodi
goodi goodi goodi
goodi goodi goodi
goodi goodi goodi
goodi goodi goodi
goodi goodi goodi
goodi goodi
good.

Lake and River Birds

More terrible than chaos,
and we stand at the edge
Of nothing. How shall we
know its purpose,
this wild bird

Leslie Norris
Blue Lightning

His father loved birds to come to his garden. He had widened the trickle of a stream that bordered this plot into two small pools, so that he could keep in comfort a pair of ancient mallards, Mr and Mrs Waddle. This morning, hearing the man's voice, they hopped out of the water and hurried loudly to him. Mrs Waddle, always the braver, marched to his feet and pecked at his brown slippers. She paused to look up, her head on one side, out of a round black eye. A yard away, Mr Waddle looked on benevolently. He was in his summer glory, his green head glossy, his speculum a trim bar of reflecting blue. James's father went off to the garage, where he kept a sack of poultry food.

It was then that a kingfisher flew in, paused above the stream, and dived. He was blue lightning, an arrow of light; his flight was electric and barbarous. He took instantly from the shallow water a small fish, stickleback or minnow, and perched on the wooden post that had held a clematis, killed by harsh frost two years back. James saw the brilliant turquoise of the bird's back, the warm chestnut breast, his sturdy beak. The kingfisher held the small fish struggling across his beak and whacked it savagely and expertly against the wood before he slid it down his throat. Then he flew, seeming to leave behind a visible echo of his flight, a streak of colour. James's father came out of the garage, holding a bowl of pellets. His ducks begged and skidded before him. He had missed the whole appearance of the kingfisher.

W.H. Davies
The Kingfisher

It was the Rainbow gave thee birth,
    And left thee all her lovely hues;
And, as her mother's name was Tears,
    So runs it in thy blood to choose
For haunts the lonely pools, and keep
In company with trees that weep.

Go you and, with such glorious hues,
    Live with proud Peacocks in green parks;
On lawns as smooth as shining glass,
    Let every feather show its marks;
Get thee on boughs and clap thy wings
Before the windows of proud kings.

Nay, lovely Bird, thou art not vain;
    Thou hast no proud ambitious mind;
I also love a quiet place
    That's green, away from all mankind;
A lonely pool, and let a tree
Sigh with her bosom over me.

GERAINT GOODWIN
Colour and Loveliness

...no one was to know that she was going to see the kingfisher. She had seen it many times from her bedroom window, flying out from the waterfall to the brook. She knew it was the kingfisher by its low drumming flight, straight as a rod, and then the final curl. But there was only one way to see a kingfisher, and that was from behind – follow its flight through. The flash of the passing bird was not enough. It was like a shooting star – the colours seemed to explode and before she had lifted her eyes it was all over. But to follow the bird through, to watch the light gather on the drumming wings and the colours glisten like so many facets, finally to blend and liquefy and so enshroud it as a nimbus... that was to see the kingfisher.

And she wanted to see the kingfisher – the colour and the loveliness of it on this first brilliant day of spring. She knew that if she climbed along the bank to the waterfall it would fly out from among the boulders, the water dripping from it and the thin spring sun lighting it.

Gerallt Jones
Geese At Gregynog

The geese have gone. There's no scarcity
of commotion on the surface of the lake: the raucous
pontificating coot on busybody rounds,
its black fuss ruffling the cosy greyness;

the wild ducks, quaa, quaa, rising in terror
and circling, flailing the rushes, raising an uproar
in the tanglewood of the island; on tranquil wing
an old buzzard, chilling on a summer evening.

No lack. But the straight-backed fleet I've watched each night
again this year, rowing trim nautical
single file through the rushes at the sunset hour,
they fledged, wings, they left. It's a sorry world!

Lacking their head-high dignity, bereaved
is a lake's civility. And the image imposed
on geese? How false! They were gentle creatures,
their progress soft and graceful across water's mirror.

At nightfall they'd walk, a cautious band,
from their browsing in the tall hay to their rightful stand
in the rushes and sword-grass, slipping so smoothly
into their element and claiming possession of a patch.

Six little ones, brown and flimsy, proud father in front
guiding, and one at the rear, every moment
keen her concern for the goslings—
a tidy organic family, a nucleus of nurture.

Over months of disturbance in a lake—crows' yakking,
jay's shriek of malice, man's two heavy feet,
they were the civilized element, the constant activity
of their care and their growth affirming continuity.

But tonight, at summer's end, winter is at hand,
its sudden forward cold a guarantee
    that I will see, next year perhaps, a springtime when
    the geese will not ever come back to the lake again.

KATE BINGHAM

Out Shooting

Muddy dogs quarter the marsh
and the snipe blow cover,
leaping up in cartwheels like a spray of knives.
You squeeze the trigger.

Little birds are easier to down.
The pellets fly out in a kind of triangle
and it only takes one to splinter a wing.
I mark exactly where it fell

and now the snipe is flapping and kicking
on the grass, frantic with pain.
I know I wanted you to fire. The palm of my hand
still hurts where my nails dug in.

FRANCIS KILVERT

Duck Merchants

Diary, 1870

...The picnic party now came from the house to the landing stage and we saw them embark and push off. The boatman said the men were dissenting ministers and he laughed at them, calling them 'duck merchants'. I asked what he meant and he said it was a regular local name for these persons – because they were fond of ducks. They had a boat load of ducks on board now at any rate and they seemed to be having good fun for we heard the girls screaming and laughing across the water.

JOSEPH P. CLANCY

Heron Music

There is air and water in it. The angularity
Of stiff legs slowly striding, wading slowly
Through the shallows. Stillness in it. The sinuosity
Of neck poised over ripples, waiting, waiting.

There is solitude in it. The singular concentration
Of eyes upon fish. Severity in it. Suddenness;
Neck a shaft, beak splitting the brook. There is
Economy in it. Precision. Satisfaction.

There is gravity in it. The stability, year after year,
Of the bracken-lined bowl of sticks in the tall tree.
Serenity in it, of wings weighing the wind
Ruffling feathers, whistling through trailing toes.

GLADYS MARY COLES

Heron In The Alyn

I follow the river, heron-seeking
where weed and nettle reign,
caught in my sorrows
and my imagined sorrows.
Flies flick and rise, torment
slow cattle. Willows trail the water
and floating celandine; maybe also Ophelia,
singing *'O, you must wear your rue*
with a difference.'

Seeking the heron
I make unexpected finds -
the sludge of a water-rat's lair,
sheep's wool a ragged veil on wire,

a tree-wound colonised by fungus –
and suddenly I see the secret bird!

Hidden in a tanglebend,
grey visitant in fish-vigil,
alert in the afternoon heat.
Such startled lift-off
of great wings, crashing
through boughs, attaining sky.

I watch the slow pulse
of its flight, the laboured ease,
diminishing into distance
with its weight of unseen freight –
my sorrows, my imagined sorrows.

VERNON WATKINS

The Heron

The cloud-backed heron will not move:
He stares into the stream.
He stands unfaltering while the gulls
And oyster-catchers scream.
He does not hear, he cannot see
The great white horses of the sea,
But fixes eyes on stillness
Below their flying team.

How long will he remain, how long
Have the grey woods been green?
The sky and the reflected sky,
Their glass he has not seen,
But silent as a speck of sand
Interpreting the sea and land,
His fall pulls down the fabric
Of all that windy scene.

Sailing with clouds and woods behind,
Pausing in leisured flight,
He stepped, alighting on a stone,
Dropped from the stars of night.
He stood there unconcerned with day,
Deaf to the tumult of the bay,
Watching a stone in water,
A fish's hidden light.

Sharp rocks drive back the breaking waves,
Confusing sea with air.
Bundles of spray blown mountain-high
Have left the shingle bare.
A shipwrecked anchor wedged by rocks,
Loosed by the thundering equinox,
Divides the herded waters,
The stallion and his mare.

Yet no distraction breaks the watch
Of that time-killing bird.
He stands unmoving on the stone;
Since dawn he has not stirred.
Calamity about him cries,
But he has fixed his golden eyes
On water's crooked tablet,
On light's reflected word.

Leslie Norris

Curlew

Dropped from the air at evening this desolate call
Mock us who listen to its delicate non-humanity.
Dogs smile, cats flatter, cows regard us all
With eyes like those of ladies in the city.

So that we transfer to them familiar human virtues
To comfort and keep us safe. But this adamant bird
With the plaintive throat and curved uneasy jaws
Crying creates a desert with a word

More terrible than chaos, and we stand at the edge
Of nothing. How shall we know its purpose, this wild bird,
Whose world is not confined by the linnets' hedge,
Whose mouth lets fly the appaling cry we heard?

Euros Bowen
The Swan

Today the art of our retreat
Is to see portents and mystery –
To see colour and sinew, the flash of white
As the bare hills of the age are visited from heaven:
His solitude swims in the quiet of the water,
A pilgrim acquainted with sedges,
And he washes the weather of the lake with his form
That (as it were) spotlights the passion
Of a soul's breath
As it goes its slow, bare way in the chill of March:
His neck became a vigil,
The immaculate arm of a hunter,
The poise there, the stance of his eye! –
And the flame of his beak plummeted down to the pool:
The mountains looked disquieted
As he resumed his glide, easing himself to the flood:
A shiver ran through his wings, then stopped,
And on a sharp beat he broke from the water:
Slowly he went, then up to the high air,
And the fire of his wings draws a soul from its cold.

DAFYDD AP GWILYM

The Swan On Syfaddon Lake

Fair swan, the lake you ride
Like white-robed abbot in your pride;
Round-foot bird of the drifted snow,
Like heavenly visitant you show.
A stately ministry is yours,
And beauty haunts your young hours.
From God's hand this day you take
Lordship over Syfaddon lake,
And two noble gifts you have
To keep you safe from the whelming wave:
Master craft in fishery –
On the wide lake could better be?–
And skill to fly on high and far
On strong wings over hill and scaur.
Your eyes discern, high overhead,
Earth's face beneath you spread,
And search all ways the watery deep,
Whose countless crop of fish you reap.
Riding the waves in stately sort
For fish to angle is your sport,
And your fishing rod, beyond compare,
'Tis your long neck, shapely and fair.
Warden you are of the round lake,
Fair-hued as the foam-flake.
Pure white through the wild waves shown;
In shirt as bright as crystal stone
And doublet all of lilies made
And flowered waistcoat you're arrayed,
With jacket wove of the wild white rose;
And your gown like honeysuckle shows.
Radiant you all fowls among,
White-cloaked bird of heaven's throng...

GWENALLT JONES

The Swan

I caught a hurried glimpse of it
While going in a train to the North;
A swan on a scrap of lake at the foot of a cliff;
And its neck was like a slim white circle
As it laid its beak in its breast.
How still the lake,
How serene the swan;
The stillness green, virginal;
The serenity light, untested,
And the solitude innocent.

And I suddenly remembered the high god of the Greeks
Taking the form of a swan to tread Leda,
And begetting two eggs;
Through the shell of one came fateful Helen,
Ancient Helen seeing in the mirror
The wrinkles on her face;
And the beauty, that cut down the young wheat of two nations,
Annihilated by the clock.

"The swan on its comely lake"
And its neck like a lucid circle:
The divine romantic love
Turned to meditative stillness:
The storms of raging, piercing passion
Turned to ripe serenity:
The marble swan on the lake bringing to mind
Images, human and disciplined, Greek.
The pure, classical swan.

Alun Llewelyn-Williams
The Swans

The summer evening when two white swans came,
    two clumsy wayfarers above the tree-tops,
    on course to the hidden, appointed time,
the final rite at the altars of the hill fell silent.

That was long ago. What graceful power
    was swept away by the incomprehensible
    tumult of their aspiration's wings,
indeed, indeed, I do not know. But when the sound died

Of their labouring journey on the world's far reaches,
    the early stars did not smile, and harsh
    the revels of the dancers in the mansion;
in a lonely marsh, their death was silent.

The Crow Family

the sun's
search finds out
the wet silk of
your gothic suit

Anna Wigley
Crow

Something un-birdlike in the immodest tilt
of your head, surprises the blood:

so near, so big, you clumsily strut
the park's nursery grass

with a brute thug's
brazen look, as if you'd snatched

from us each muddy ditch
and daisy patch, that now

proved paltry loot.
Waddling bandy feet

you stroll for a moment the
high path, like a boozer

shameless of his gut.
Then you're off

bouncing on wires across grass,
spearing your next kebab.

For a chaser there's nuts
and a nutcracker fence.

The sun's search finds out the
wet silk of your Gothic suit

as at last you transform yourself,
suddenly taking flight,

a great ragged shape
thrashing the air like a stubborn mule,

the fan of your radiant wing
shaking the black blades out.

FRANCIS KILVERT
Spoiling Everything

Diary, 1870
On Easter Day all the young people come out in something new and bright like butterflies. It is almost part of their religion to wear something new on this day. It was an old saying that if you don't wear something new on Easter Day the crows will spoil everything you have on.

HUW MENAI
Rooks
(December)

Gleaners of grain they did not sow
Four rooks are standing in a row
Upon a rusty, upturned plough,
Whose blunted shares now wear a cloak
As brown as the brown earth they broke,
Far too well-fed to know unrest –
Each beak reclining on each breast,
When every bulging gizzard hath
Known surfeit of the aftermath,
Mute, living monuments are these
Of even darker mysteries,
In solemn conclave here, alone,
When Nature's fasting to the bone,
And I'd give much to understand
What quiet business they've in hand,

Perhaps a search might in them find
Spirits of Plato and his kind
Flown from Elysian fields to gaze
On frosted stubble and lean days;
Might know regret for shots which took
Old Pythagoras for a rook.
And on this Winter day so fine
How brilliantly their black coats shine;
Four lovely stars whose lustre strewn
A midnight maketh of blue noon,
And sensing some foul brute in man,
(Not the divinity in his plan).
They give to sturdy wings their span,
And fly away, as stars would fly,
If they had wings when man goes by.

GREG HILL

Jackdaw

That was the year they built in our chimney supplying
twigs for kindling direct to the laid fire
(when people say the smoke keeps down their fleas
and the heat is a comfort in the nest,
do they rationalise or know what they can't prove?)

One day, when we'd stopped lighting fires,
there was a call of *Mam, Dad, come and look*
and Mali hovered by the door, pointing
to the chick in a pile of soot on the clean hearth
regarding us with a slant eye. Could it fly?

We took it upstairs and put it out of the landing window
on the ridge of the extension roof. It seemed happy
enough, shook its wings, hopped, then sat there cheeping.
Next time we looked it was gone. But the next

day there was a flutter and a fall of soot
from the chimney and there, again, was a dark bird
in the dark hole of the fire place. A familiar
piece of mystery visiting the safe predictability
of our living room. If it was the same one

(as we thought) why did it come – did it bring
omens, good or bad luck or a message
from the vital pulse and strangeness of what we call
the natural world? Did it accuse us of desertion?
Thoughts are one thing, the need for action another

so why can I not remember what we did then
but only a bird sitting there, happier in our hearth
than in the crowded nest, looking so pleased with itself?
By now it is an image in memory, a token of wildness
come close but one I can't exchange for knowledge:

An object as dark as a jackdaw's feathers
or the soot in a chimney dims the clear outline
of the fire frame; like a jig-saw piece from another puzzle
it doesn't fit any space I have for it
but sits all the same waiting to find its place.

Richard Poole

Circles

Black upon azure, jackdaws wheel
above broken turrets of grey stone;
on loan from earth to sky, they return
when the fancy takes them, again feel
earthliness under their clawed toes.
So things go back to their origins –
creatures of feather, bone and skin
to the muck from which they arose.

Why cavil at simplicity,
the closing of the necessary circle?
Life cannot escape symmetry:
puddles vanish in sunlight, icicles
drip reluctant, lucid tears. They coldly
splash your childish hands, you drink them thoughtlessly.

Tom Earley

Jackdaw

Mischievous, they say, as a monkey,
Thieving as a magpie, meddlesome
As a child of two, but I have never
Found you so. The most I've seen
You take was wool for your nest
From a cud-chewing, complacent sheep.
I find you well-behaved and wonder
How your evil reputation arose.
I've never known your kind in England;
There you would seem alien, out of place.
But here in this mining village I see
Your relatives in all the streets, one pair
To every chimney. What do you eat
In this hungry place? Do you live on smoke?
I've seen you on the mountain, perched
On the back of a consenting ewe,
Picking tics from her fleece. But here
It's either the crumbs from the poor
Man's table or the flies. Normally
A quiet bird with your occasional
Low monosyllabic unraucous caw,
When you quarrel with your wife
You stand across your chimney pot
Like all eloquent Welsh preacher
Leaning out of the loud pulpit
In the holy passion of his *hwyl.*

Then I can well believe you could
Be taught human speech and I know,
Monoglot, that you would speak Welsh.

Jean Earle
The Jackdaw

A chancy morning, after rain.

Cot-child opening
To differences in light, words –

Which clump together now
Muscular knots, lifting the infant head,
All eyes, all ears.

A voice in the lane,
Calling through misted sun.
'The jackdaw's dead.'

Never to know whose voice,
Which bird; that lane
Viewed from a window only.

No one there.

Often, piercing the long life's
Deep experience
Of rain silvering a bright sun

These claps: without any reference
To what's being said, what's on...
Like a spoke in a wheel,
Suddenly it squeaks
Out of a radiant fog.

"The jackdaw's dead."

JIM PERRIN
This Wildest of Birds

In our century and urban societies we are so unused to encounters with wild creatures. Compare the modern Welsh poet Robert Williams Parry's taut surprise at his meeting with a fox, and the way it slips out of his sight '*megis seren wib*' ('like a shooting star') in the famous sonnet, with his great precursor Dafydd ap Gwilym's laddishly familiar apostrophizing of the same animal six hundred years earlier:

Gwr yw ef a garai iar,
A choeg edn, a chig adar.

(He's a fellow who loves the hens
And stupid fowl, and flesh of birds.)

So there was delight in this tamed setting at being in so close proximity to a creature which is, for me, the apotheosis of wildness. And that sense I have of the raven is not just one of those anti-civilization compensatory impulses like that of Williams Parry towards the fox. It is more primitive than that. Remember the Morrigan, the shape-shifting raven-goddess of slaughter in Irish mythology, and how, in the *Tain Bo Cuailnge* she settles on a standing stone and tells matters to the Brown Bull: of hosts gathering to certain slaughter, of the raven ravenous among corpses of men, of affliction and outcry and war everlasting, raging over Cuailnge with the deaths of sons, the deaths of kinsmen, death upon death, until the Bull, maddened, casts off restraint and rages uncontrollably through the land. Remember the Morrigan's temptation, in the guise of King Buan's daughter, of Cuchulain in the same epic, her seductive guiles and desire for love before his battles with Loch's brother and Loch himself. I remembered them as I watched this wildest of birds, this inhabitant of the wildest places, in perfect stillness from twenty feet away, a distance close enough for me to see the dark brown iris of its eye, the dark grey interior of its bill. And it was aware of my presence as another creature. It began to communicate with me. At first, its gestures were aggresive, the wings drooped on either side, tail fanned, bill snapping, and a guttural, metallic note growled out at me. But then it began to relax, the ruffled feathers on legs and head smoothed down, it preened and pecked at the branch, tilted its head straight up in a gesture of supplication or appeasement, looked away and then looked round again, squatted low on the branch with wings half open and tail feathers held straight and quivering, and all the time with a rather soft and musical rolling call to me, and by all of this I was quite entranced.

But as I watched, and as my mind drifted across the terrible images of mythology – the prophetess of slaughter, the seductress of warriors, the washer at the ford – I noticed another aspect of the bird, which caused it to shift in my perception a degree away from the surprising-but still understandable. For a thickness of perhaps two inches around its entire body – head, legs, wings, tail – and moving with it whenever it moved, was a bright, translucent violet aura. Just that. I have no explanation for it. I took off my glasses in case it was an effect produced by refraction through their lenses. The aura remained. I changed my angle of view. The aura persisted as the raven responded to this new game. Suddenly, behind me, a blonde-haired woman appeared. The raven flew away, taking its aura and presence with it.

The woman and I exchanged greetings. 'You must be King Buan's daughter,' I said to her, and walked away in silent, puzzled laughter. But this is a prosaic ending, and beyond it came the phase of making friends with ravens. So that now, in my garden, the young of last year's brood call from the wire and feed from my hand.

JEAN EARLE
Llansteffan Shore

Over the vast of silver mud,
Silence. The tide has gone
Very far out. Two married ravens
Wait its return.

Our drift-fire wavers, smoking
The warm, soft grey air.
On their accustomed stone, the two birds
Shimmer to four.

This is a place to take home
As a salve. It can be put on a wound,
It finds keys
To a shut door.

Silver; and grey. The turned tide
Sighs from Cefn Sidan.
Peace: and the reassuring
Life-style of ravens...

GILLIAN CLARKE
Choughs

I follow you downhill to the edge
My feet taking as naturally as yours
To a sideways tread, finding footholds
Easily in the turf, accustomed
As we are to a sloping country.

The cliffs buttress the bay's curve to the north
And here drop sheer and sudden to the sea.
The choughs plummet from sight then ride
The updraught of the cliffs' mild yellow
Light, fold, fall with closed wings from the sky.

At the last moment as in unison they turn
A ripcord of the wind is pulled in time.
He gives her food and the saliva
Of his red mouth, draws her black feathers, sweet
As shining grass across his bill.

Rare birds that pair for life. There they go
Divebombing the marbled wave a yard
Above the spray. Wings flick open
A stoop away
From the drawn teeth of the sea.

Larks

... I hear the lark ascend, His rash-fresh re-winded new skeined score, In crisps of curl off wild winch whirl

CHRISTOPHER MEREDITH
Larks

Snow retracts in hollows
Above the adit mouth which
Blows rank air under larks climbing.

Houses without people
Lose all sense of self-respect:
Mosses etch the mortar, slates fall

And plaster falls from laths.
The piebald hill shrugs off snow,
Shrugs off people and the walls

Give up and tumble. Cars
Come and callers sup the past
And leave. To give up and be sad,

Like stones, is so easy
Though this is scarcely even sad –
Just random, as where weeds will grow.

Like winddriven midges
We came, clung a moment, went
When economics belched up the drift

With the reek of fear.
Matter is so unheeding
Blame needn't taint the taste of loss.

Yet over Troedrhiwgwair
Larks nail the light with hammered air
Climbing, will-sustained, beyond sight.

Tom Earley
Lark

Helicopter of the hill,
with your vertical take-
off and controlled poise
as you climb, you make
the mountain shrill
with your noise.

Coming in to land,
you drop suddenly
straight as a stone
to meet the ground
but not directly
to your home.

You leave the air
through cold couch-grass
and wind-blown heather
so none know whether
you merely pass
or live there.

If put to the test
when I was young,
I could find the nest
of any species among
the birds of Wales
except yours.

Gerard Manley Hopkins
The Sea And The Skylark

On ear and ear two noises too old to end
  Trench – right, the tide that ramps against the shore;
  With a flood or a fall, low lull-off or all roar,
Frequenting there while moon shall wear and wend.

Left hand, off land, I hear the lark ascend,
  His rash-fresh re-winded new skeined score
  In crisps of curl off wild winch whirl, and pour
And pelt music, till none's to spill nor spend.

How these two shine this shallow and frail town!
  How ring right out our sordid turbid time,
Being pure! We, life's pride and cared-for crown,

  Have lost that cheer and charm of earth's past prime:
Our make and making break, are breaking, down
  To man's last dust, drain fast towards man's first slime.

Bobi Jones
Skylark

I would swear the sun split with singing.
Was it not from his tongue a throng of notes
Leapt, the chime of his beam upon them,
Like bells of water exploding through glass?

In the eloquent river nettles and broom
Sunbathed, and the gardens of houses.
But it's a bird there a blacksmith welding
Man and firmament in a furnace of praise.

Cage Birds

… his colours as
loud as his voice –
screeching red,
squawking blue

Paul Groves
Parrots

The parrot is sure of something. He has
a copywriter's tie for a body. He holds
his own at parties, high in the trees,
impressing all the flappers. His whole family
are show-offs; they tend to get
above themselves, preening in the lianas,
bowling through hot mist like an extrovert
leaving a Turkish bath. I envy
their composure, the way they turn
jungles into tunnels of love, the way
they fuss and prance like a child storming
a gem-box. All are egregiously overdressed:
pantomime dames one minute, foppish gallery
directors the next. And what have they
to be proud of? A voice like a chain saw,
gaudy sequin eyes, a bill as bent
as the delivery of a leg-spinner.
As for their haunts, these are venomous,
sweaty, vertiginous, decidedly seedy.
And yet, given the dourness of sloths,
the stolidness of capybaras, it is refreshing
to consider the existence of parrots, even if,
occasionally, they become one cocktail too many.

Gwyn Thomas
Parrot

A bird, a bird that has been
Stumbling through pots full of paint
So that his colour's as loud as his voice –
Screeching red, squawking blue,
A shower of shouting grating green,

Besides technicolour swearing and blasting.
He's an exploding palette of a bird
A jabbering coloured window
With a great yellow sun
Struggling to get out of him
Through the joyous panes of his feathers.

MARGIAD EVANS

Death

(Song of a Cage-Bird)

A colder wind along the passage blew –
I felt it too –
And she, she was dying.
The candle was dipping, her fist was untying.

I must die too.

I saw her soul come through
Her body like a hand through bars...

I must go too.

No-one to give me sup or seed
Or sprig of garden weed...

I must die too.

So from this little window plot of stars
I must go too.

HARRI WEBB
Our Budgie

Our budgie lives in a cage of wire
Equipped to please his each desire,
He has a little ladder to climb
And he's up and down it all the time.
And a little mirror in which he peeps
As he utters his self-admiring cheeps,
And two little pink plastic budgie mates
Whom he sometimes loves and sometimes hates.
And a little bell all made of tin
On which he makes a merry din.
Though sometimes, when things aren't going well,
He hides his head inside the bell.
His feathers are a brilliant green
And take most of his time to preen,
His speech is limited and blurred
But he doesn't do badly, for a bird.
And though he can but poorly talk
If you ignore him he'll squawk and squawk
And fly into a fearful rage
And rattle the bars of his pretty cage,
But he won't get out, he'll never try it,
And a cloth on the cage will keep him quiet.

This futile bird, it seems to me,
Would make a perfect Welsh M.P.

Miscellany

Let us celebrate
the single-cloaked
beings
Content in
their coats of fur and
feathers...

George Owen
This Odious Bird

Nevarne is the greatest and largest parishe in the Sheere and taketh name of the ryver Nevarne wch runneth well neere throw the myddest of the same.

In Welsh it is called *Inhyver* and in old tyme was dedicated to the bryttifhe Saint called *Sainct Burnaghe* whose festifalle day is yet dulie observed within this and dyverse other parishes with noe smale solempnitie the seaventh of April, on wch day yt is wth us said the Cocow first beginneth to tune her laye. I might well here omytt an old report freshe as yet of this odiouse bird that in the old world the parishe priest would not beginne Masse in this parishe untill this bird (called the Citizens ambassador) had first appeared and begann her note upon a stone called Saint Burnaghes stone being a stone curiouslie wrought with sondrie sortes of knottes standing upright in the Churcheyarde of this parishe, and one yere stayeinge verey longue and the priest and people expecting her accustomed cominge (for I accompt this byrd of the feminyne gender) cam at last and lightinge upon the said stone her accustomed preaching place and being scarse able once to sounde the note upon the said stone presentlie fell downe dead. This religiouse tale althoughe yt Concerne in some sorte Churche matters you may eyther beleave or not without perill of damnation.

Robin Gwyndaf
The Cuckoos of Risca

The people of Risca decided that they would like to have fine weather all the year round. They had noticed that it was always sunny when the cuckoo visited their town, thus concluding that the cuckoo was responsible for it. They planned, therefore, to keep the bird throughout the year and built high hedges all round the town. The cuckoo arrived, but when it was time to leave it just flew over the hedges, leaving the innocent people of Risca very angry with themselves that they had not built the hedges a little higher! And that is why the inhabitants of the town received the nickname 'The Cuckoos of Risca.'

This is an international folk tale, associated also, for example, with 'The Cuckoos of Dolwyddelan', Gwynedd, North Wales. In England the best known version relates to the 'Cuckoos of Pent.'

CLYDE HOLMES

Cuckoo

Echoes himself –

sounding out
his isolation
with tuneful hiccuping.

Patrols for pipits.
Nests bombed by eggs –

brittle explosions
of his own gawky flesh.

JOHN GURNEY

The Swift

Something was recovered, suddenly.
The weather had developed, and the wind
had fanned its wings, and driven on the rain
that poured down without pause, as night and day,
it washed away the insects from the air,
thus weakening the swifts. Overtired,
unable to avoid the northern air,
to skim beyond the outskirts of the storm
outwitting its dark thunders, gliding past
its blue down-burning lightnings, all the swifts

flew lower in the evening, clutched our walls
to hang like stencilled shadows. One alone
had fallen to our doorstep, where it lay,
immobile, stretched, just breathing, with its head
set quietly on the leather of your shoe
as if it felt the heat, the human warmth
that flowed out from your body. You had stopped.
You stared down at the bird in disbelief.
Its dark brown wings were stiff as scimitars
and wider than a kestrel's, glimmering
in glassy dark translucence as it kept
one eye unclosed, the other flickering
beneath its shutting lid, as if it held
its consciousness half-open. Now at last
its movements had been stilled, its restlessness,
that scribbled, mad agraphia of its flight,
scarce seen, but gone away, a vanishing,
as fleeting as the quality of time,
a quivering of meaning. And its calls
that peeted down the street, between the trees
like whistles blown at spirits, or the sounds
of scrying-stones transfigured by the wind
were silenced, as submissively he stretched
where yesterday the nestlings had been dropped
unfledged, and bald, half-naked. Then you bent,
lifted him, and set him to your breast,
held him in the warm skin of your palms
as if cupped in a nest, his tight beak shut,
unwilling then to open, as you shared
the silence of his blissful timelessness
in absolute absorption, rested in
the certainty of presence, suddenly
at one, and self-sufficient. But he moved:
grasped you with his sharply needled claws,
re-opened then the great gape of his throat,
the wide yawn made for grazing at the flies
that glittered in the meadows of the air,
unclosing then the black balls of his eyes

that scanned you like a hawk, a predator,
alive again, desiring. So you knelt:
took him to the window, to the grass,
the movement of the breeze, the swaying boughs
that pricked him into action, as he moved,
flashed with an activity of wings
that took off in a straight low-level flight
that banked then through the garden, cleared the wall,
rose up past the black roof of the barn
to climb off through the evening, flittering
a last shade in the twilight. And at night,
alone now in the stillness of the room,
you stare up at the glass waste of the stars
imagining activity, your eyes
still searching for a movement, for a glide,
a body like an arrow in a bow
that sleeps upon the wing, some two miles high,
alive there with the young unmated males
untroubled by the dark shade of the earth,
illumined by the full face of the moon.

GLYN JONES
Swifts

Shut-winged fish, brown as mushroom,
The sweet, hedge-hurdling swifts, zoom
Over waterfalls of wind.
I salute all those lick-finned,
Dusky-bladed air-cutters.
Could you weave words as taut, sirs,
As those swifts', great *cywydd* kings,
Swart basketry of swoopings?

VERNON WATKINS

Swallows

Artists are swallows
Building a nesting-place of earth.
The far each follows,
Returning always to his place of birth.

Welsh ambassadors,
Stubborn of instinct, mould in clay
The travelled shores,
And break down colours from an earlier day.

Vision lifts the mind,
Turning their swallows' flight to grace.
In eaves they find,
But nowhere on the ground, a settled place.

Linked in heart and cry,
They weave a lost age. Devious wings
Trace in crossed sky
A timeless writing, strict as tightened strings.

Bow and harpstring both
Sound where a seawave hits the sand.
Eager and loth,
The two vibrations answer the one hand.

Savage history throws
Chance to the winds and cuts the thread.
Iron and rose
Point recollection, trim the arrowhead.

Here Aneirin drew
Anguish from stone for youth cut down.
Here Llywarch threw
Remorse at Death, who took his every son.

Thought and arrow once
Flew from the rockhead's ambush. Now
Those fallen sons
Haunt the bleak furrows, interrupt the plough.

Still Taliesin stays,
Touching, more near than all we know,
The pulse of praise,
Deeper, more strong, than string of harp or bow.

Sword and rattling shield
Tell, in plucked verse, how sharp-edged war
Struck, in the field.
Without Christ's birth how vain Earth's mornings are.

These, whose flight is toil,
Live but to praise the elusive mark;
Whether in oil,
Sculpture, verse, music, keen wings cut through dark.

Storm will but restore
The wings' true balance. Faith can make
Love's metaphor
Strong, to give time more truth, the more time take.

MIKE JENKINS
Martins

A line of martins
bring to the wire
their abrupt, reed-splitting
calls. Each tick
they weed from their feathers
is a phrase to repeat.

They look so balanced there,
the sun giving a tulip's shine.
Their wings spread suddenly
as if you could see petals emerging
in a second. They stretch
the bounds of your sight
as they dart down a chasm
of flies above the stream.

Returning to the wire
they cut contours in the air
with scythe-shaped wings.
Mid-air contact, when flies caught
are planted from beak to beak,
sends two songs together,
their seedbursts shaking open wings.

Look closer: the martin's thumb of a head
is animated by signals, as if vibrations
from the wire had become the steady drone
of insects, a burr catching its eyes.
It is hard to think of this bird
cupped in a close cave of a nest,
when you have seen it garden
the air with its feeding flight.

Charles Tunnicliffe
A Well Dressed Bird

We had caught a glimpse of a sunlit flock of birds swooping down to a field farther along the road so, as much will have more, thither we went, and saw that the recently harrowed field held a flock of Golden Plover. Golden they were, but also very black and white, a flock of approximately four hundred birds, all of the Northern race. The most immaculate of them appeared as black birds each clothed with a white-edged golden shawl which fitted over the head and fell behind the cheek to be brought forward and loosely fastened down the breast, thus attired, the others, though most had the white edge to the shawl, had brown or pale buff cheeks and some white feathers spotting the black breast. W. and I agreed that the Northern Golden Plover in breeding plumage is in the topmost rank of well-dressed birds.

On the field there were two pairs of resident Lapwings, and the cock birds, between the occupations of making scrapes in the brown earth, and displaying to their hens, flew playfully above their Golden cousins and, stooping here and there, caused individuals to crouch or take wing; or again a Lapwing would suddenly run in where the flock of Goldens was thickest and menace whichever bird was nearest to him putting one after another to flight. Compared with the quick sharp-winged Northerns the Lapwings looked big and clumsy, with their broad-ended wings beating once where those of the Goldens flickered three or four times.

When the nearest birds were so close to the road that they were out of the focus of my telescope a passing bus caused the whole flock to take wing and we thought that this was the end of our watching. The birds wheeled about the confines of the field in ever-changing formation, one part of the flock at times seeming to pour down through the other. One moment golden backs only were to be seen, the next the silver and black undersides. Soon it became obvious that the plover were reluctant to leave the field, and after several undecided swoops almost to ground level the whole flock wheeled and came round heads to wind. On set wings they glided down, then, with a silvery flickering of wings beautiful to watch the host ceased its forward progress and delicately touched ground, the last birds to alight flashing this way and that to avoid a landing on the backs of those below. When all wings were closed the compact group of birds was almost invisible against the brown earth, except for those white fringes to their shawls which gleamed like a series of white question marks. Twice more they were put to wing, once by two dogs and again by a passing motor lorry, but each time they returned to the same spot with the same exquisite manoeuvre.

Bryn Griffiths

Starlings

Starlings at dusk pour across
the dull beacon of the distant sun.

A high crying, cold as winter
in the day's dark metal, they spin,

Eddy and spill down towards
the horizon's walking throng of trees.

This fist of birds, flashing black
against the sky's red warning,

batters through the wooden veins
and tells the buds of coming summer.

The slow sap, thick with a season's sleep,
quickens with the clashing song

of the driven starlings, stirs
the sluggish branches to tell

the buried roots of Spring...
And yet time hangs like a dead fruit.

Who knows this cycled secret
of spinning birds and sensing trees?

Who hears the signals sounding there?
Only blind eyes see the breaking year!

The soundless voice that tells the trees,
the wheeling arm that swings

this black fist of starlings, is rooted
in the ten million years that hover here.

Acknowledgements

Acknowledgements are due to the following for permission to include work in this anthology.

John Barnie: 'How to Watch Birds' by permission of the author, extract from *The Confirmation* (Gomer, 1992), 'That Summer', unpublished, by permission of the author; **Glenda Beagan:** extract from 'The Last Thrush' from *The Medlar Tree* (Seren, 1992); Ron Berry: extract from *Peregrine Watching* (Gomer, 1987), extract from 'Hunters and Hunted' by permission of the Estate of Ron Berry; **Ruth Bidgood:** 'Blue Tit Feeding' from *The Fluent Moment* (Seren, 1996); **Alison Bielski:** 'The Birds' by permission of the author; **Kate Bingham:** 'Out Shooting' from *Cohabitation* (Seren, 1998); **Euros Bowen:** 'Winged in Gold' and 'The Gull' translated by the poet, 'The Nightingale' translated by R Gerallt Jones in *The Poetry of Wales 1930-1970* (Gomer, 1974); **Duncan Bush**: extract from 'The Snowy Owl' from *Drawing Down the Moon* (Seren 1996); **Vuyelwa Carlin:** 'Icarus' from *How We Dream of the Dead* (Seren, 1995), 'Birdsong' from *Marble Sky* (Seren, 2002); **Phil Carradice**: extract from *The Isle of Avalon* (1999) by permission of the author; **Brenda Chamberlain**: extract from *Tide-race* (Seren, 1987 edition) by permission of the Estate of Brenda Chamberlain; **Alan Cilie:** 'Kestrel' translated by Joseph P. Clancy in *Twentieth Century Welsh Poems* (Gomer, 1983); **Anne Cluysenaar**: 'The Wagtail' by permission of the author; **Gillian Clarke:** 'Wild Sound', 'Blodeuwedd', 'Choughs' and 'Mass of Birds' by permission of Carcanet Press; **Gladys Mary Coles**: 'Augury' and 'Heron in the Alyn' by permission of the author; **William Condry**: extract from *The Natural History of Wales* (Collins, 1981), extract from *Wildlife, My Life* (Gomer, 1995); **Tony Curtis**: 'Pembrokeshire Buzzards' from *Taken for earls* (Poetry Wales Press, 1993); **Bryan Martin Davies:** 'Lleu' is translated by R. Gerallt Jones in *The Poetry of Wales 1930-1970* (Gomer, 1974); **Idris Davies** 'Send out your homing pigeons, Dai' from *Collected Poems* (University of Wales Press, 1994) by permission of the Estate of Idris Davies; **John Davies:** 'Ray's Bird' from *Dirt Roads* (Seren, 1997); 'The Swift', unpublished; **Jean Earle**: 'Dancing Pheasants' and 'The Jackdaw' from *Selected Poems* (Seren, 1990), 'Llansteffan Shore' from *The Sun in the West* (Seren,

1995); **Menna Elfyn**: 'A Bird in the Hand' from *Eucalyptus* (Gomer, 1995); **Christine Evans**: 'Gannets' by permission of the author; **Margiad Evans**: extract 1 from 'A Party for the Nightingale' (Welsh Review, 1947), extract 2 from *Autobiography* (Blackwell, 1943), 'Death' and 'A Sparrow Singing' from *Poems from Obscurity* (Andrew Dakers, 1947); **Peter Finch**: 'Scaring Hens' from *Selected Poems* (Poetry Wales Press, 1987); **Catherine Fisher**: 'Blodeuwedd' from *Altered States* (Seren, 1999); **Alan Garner**: extract from *The Owl Service* (Puffin Books, 1969); **Geraint Goodwin**: extract from *The Heyday in the Blood* (Cape, 1969) by permission of the Goodwin Estate; **Paul Groves**: 'Parrots' from *Academe* (Poetry Wales Press, 1988); **Peter Gruffydd**: 'Burial of Strange Birds' first published in the New Welsh Review; **John Gurney**: 'The Swift' appeared in *Poetry Wales: 25 Years* (Poetry Wales Press, 1990); **Gwenallt**: 'The Swan' translated by Joseph P. Clancy in *Twentieth Century Welsh Poems* (Gomer, 1983); **Greg Hill**: 'The Jackdaw' appears by permission of the author; **Clyde Holmes**: 'Cuckoo' from *Skywalks* (Gwasg Carreg Gwlach, 1998); **Emyr Humphreys**: 'Branwen's Starling' and 'Turkeys in Wales' from *Collected Poems* (UWP, 1999); **Elin ap Hywel**: 'Owl Report' from *A Celtic Resurgence* (New Native Press, 1997); **Mike Jenkins**: 'Red Kite over Heol Nanteos' and 'Diver Bird' from *This House, My Ghetto* (Seren, 1995), 'Martins' from *The Common Land* (Poetry Wales Press, 1980), 'Odd Bird' by permission of the author; **R. Gerallt Jones**: 'Geese at Gregynog' translated by Joseph P. Clancy in *Twentieth Century Welsh Poems* (Gomer, 1983); **Gwilym R. Jones:** 'Psalm to the Creatures' translated by Joseph P. Clancy in *Twentieth Century Welsh Poems* (Gomer, 1983); **Glyn Jones**: 'Esyllt', 'Dafydd's Seagull and the West Wind', 'The Seagull', 'Swifts' all from *Selected Poems* (Poetry Wales Press, 1988) by permission of the Estate of Glyn Jones; **Huw Jones**: 'Old Austin' by permission of the author; **Hilary Llewellyn-Williams**: 'Hunting the Wren' from *The Tree Calendar* (Poetry Wales Press, 1987); **Alan Llwyd**: 'The Geese' is translated by the author; **Alun Llywelyn-Williams**: 'The Swan' translated by Joseph P. Clancy in *Twentieth Century Welsh Poems* (Gomer, 1983); **Eiluned Lewis**: extract from *Dew in the Grass* (Baydell Press, 1984); **Gwyneth Lewis:** 'Birds', 'Woods', 'Red Kites at Tregaron' from *Parables and Fables* (Bloodaxe Books, 1995); **J.D. Mallinson**: 'Bird-Watching in Wales' was published in the *New Welsh Review*; **Roland**

Mathias: 'Hawks' from *Burning Brambles* (Gomer, 1983); **Christopher Meredith**: extract from *Griffri* (Seren, 1991), 'Larks' from *Snaring Heaven* (Poetry Wales Press, 1990); **Kathy Miles**: 'Woman of Flowers' from *The Rocking Stone* (Poetry Wales Press, 1988); **T.E. Nicholas**: 'The Sparrow' translated by Joseph P. Clancy in *Twentieth Century Welsh Poems* (Gomer, 1983); **Leslie Norris:** 'Owls', 'Barn Owl', 'Buzzard', 'Curlew', 'Nightingales' all from *Collected Poems* (Seren, 1996), extracts from 'A Flight of Geese' and 'The Kingfisher' from *Collected Stories* (Seren, 1996); John Ormond: 'Homing Pigeons' from *Selected Poems* (Poetry Wales Press, 1987); **T.H. Parry-Williams**: 'Owl' translated by Joseph P. Clancy in *Twentieth Century Welsh Poems* (Gomer, 1983); **Jim Perrin**: extract from *A Sense of Place* (Penguin, 1998); **Richard Poole**: 'Circles' from *Autobiographies and Explanations* (Headland, 1994); **Sheenagh Pugh**: 'The Haggard and the Falconer' from *Selected Poems* (Seren, 1990); **Frances Sackett:** 'Dream of Birds' from *The Hand Glass* (Seren, 1994); **Anne Stevenson**: 'Gannets Diving' from *The Fiction Makers* (OUP, 1981); **Dylan Thomas**: 'Over Sir John's Hill' from *Collected Poems* (Dent, 1971) by permission of David Higham Associates; **Gwyn Thomas**: 'Birds' translated by R Gerallt Jones in *The Poetry of Wales 1930-1970* (Gomer, 1974), 'Seagulls' translated by Joseph P. Clancy in *Twentieth Century Welsh Poems* (Gomer, 1983), 'Parrots' translated by the poet; **R.S. Thomas:** 'A Crown' 'Inextinguishable' and 'Miraculous Lives' from *Autobiographies* (Orion, 1998), 'Unity' from *Selected Prose* (Poetry Wales Press, 1983), 'A Species' uncollected, 'Sea-Watching', 'Barn Owl', 'A Blackbird Singing' from *Collected Poems* (Dent, 1993); **John Powell Ward:** 'The Dreaming' from *The Clearing* (Poetry Wales Press, 1984); **Vernon Watkins**: 'Kestrel', 'The Heron' and 'Swallows' all from *Collected Poems* (Golgonooza Press, 1986); **Harri Webb**: 'The Nightingales' and 'Our Budgie' from *Collected Poems* (Gomer, 1995) by permission of the Estate of Harri Webb; **Meic Stephens**: 'Owl', by permission of the author; **R. Williams Parry**: 'The Owls' translated by Joseph P. Clancy in *Twentieth Century Welsh Poems* (Gomer, 1983) **Anna Wigley:** 'Duck Shooting' and 'Crow' from *The Bird Hospital* (Gomer, 2002)

Every effort has been made to contact the copyright holders of the contents of this anthology.

About the Editor

Dewi Roberts lives in Denbighshire and is one of Wales' foremost anthologisers. His publications include *Christmas in Wales* and *A Clwyd Anthology*, and a travel book, *The Land of Old Renown*. He is an essayist and reviewer for a number of publications. Apart from literature his main interest is local history.